A TRAGEDY
BY
AUNTIE ROBYNAN

A Tragedy is purely fiction; any relevance to any persons either living or deceased is strictly coincidental.

Copyright information available upon request.

ISBN 978-1-61658-243-2

A SPECIAL THANKS TO ALMIGHTY GOD, TO PASTOR GRANT AND THE ENTIRE ZION HOPE FAMILY, THE KINGDOM SISTERS, A VERY VERY SPECIAL THANKS TO MINISTER VINITA THOMPSON WHO CONSTANTLY INSPIRES ME TO BE THE BEST AT ANY AND EVERYTHING THAT I SHOW INTREST IN, TO MY MOM, SISTERS AND BROTHERS AND ALL MY COUSINS AND EXTENDED FAMILY AND ALL MY CHILDREN.

THIS BOOK IS DEDICATED TO MY PRECIOUS GRANDAUGHTER
KHLO'E

DIALOGUE;

'Terri wake up I screamed into the phone. 'No Janice she replied, I don't want to wake up this early on Saturday morning. I work hard all week for this day, she added. I work hard also, I said. Finally Terri comes to life and says, ok, I'm up, are you happy? Hell no, I'm not happy, I answer back. Do you think that I would be up calling you this early if I was happy? Please, Terri said, tell me that you are not waking me up for Derrick and his bullshit. What does that matter, I ask? You're my best friend, so you have to be here for me no matter what. I'm here, Janice; she says. I'm just sleepy because this baby kept me up all night. I told her that I just wanted her to know what I was about to do just in case something happened to me. What in the hell, are you about to do, she asked? I'm about to take all of Derrick's things over to his parent's house, I said. Why would you do that, she asked? I told her to wake the hell up and listen, so that I could tell her. I asked her if she remembered last night when I told her

that I was going to that new bar that just opened up downtown for a drink after work; she told me that she did. Well anyway I continued a couple of my co-workers and I went. There sitting at the bar, was the finest man that I've ever saw in my life. He was about six feet, two or three, light brown eyes, light complected and his hair was jet black, short and curly. His side burns we're trimmed so handsomely. Terri stopped me in mid conversation, yelling for me to get to the point. I told her that I was getting there if she would just shut her big mouth up. Anyway I continued, he approached me and we got to kicking it right? Once again Terri yelled for me to get to the point. Well, I continued again totally ignoring her. We decided that we would go out and grab a bite to eat. I kind of felt guilty, because I have a man. I felt as if I was being very unfaithful. What man Terri asked?
Don't start Terri, I say. She said that she wasn't starting anything, she just didn't like the way that I was letting Derrick ruin my life, that's all. I told her that she was absolutely right. Hell no! Terri yells sarcastically, you did not just tell me that I was right, what the hell is really going on? This has really got to be deep. Are you going to let me talk, I asked as I lose control for the hundredth time in the last six hours, and break out in tears. Why are you crying Janice, Terri asks? I told her to just forget that I even called. Forget my ass, she said finally sounding awake. What in the world is going on here, she asked? Once again I started to speak. As I was saying, I started to feel guilty about what I was doing, so I canceled out. Dumb ass, Terri yelled! Whatever, I said right back at her. I was about to get out of his car and into my own, when up drives Derrick. Oh shit; did he see you, she asked? No, I answered. I ducked backed into Marvin's car to wait for Derrick to enter the club so that I could leave. Marvin that's the guys name, wanted to know why I'm acting so strange by now. I told him that the guy that just pulled up was my boyfriend. Marvin started laughing and asked me was I serious? Why would I lie about something like that, I asked? That guy he says couldn't be your boyfriend. Why is that I

asked? Because that guy he says, is about to become my brother in law. How in the hell is Derrick becoming your brother in law, I ask? Are you trying to tell me that he's fucking around with your sister or something? No sweetie I don't have a sister he replied, Derrick Geter is my brother's fiancé. What the fuck did you just say, Terri screamed? You heard what I said, anyway I'm shocked as hell, but I manage to stay calm or at least pretend that I am. Derrick goes in the club, I get out and go to my car in shock, just as I'm about to start my ignition, I see Derrick come back out of the club and appear to be looking for someone. About five minutes later this black Mercedes pulls up and this good looking guy that I would have sworn was Marvin (the guy I had just met inside the club) steps out. The only reason that I knew it wasn't Marvin was the fact that the clothes were different. He was the same height as Marvin about six feet two or three, with the same light complexion. What happened then, Terri asked? This you will not believe I say, Derrick walks right up to this man and kisses him right in the mouth, the same way he kisses me. Oh my God Janice, Terri replies I will be there in five minutes girl this shit is crazy. That's ok, I say I don't want to deal with this right now and on top of that he didn't come home last night that's why I'm taking his things to his parents home. Oh no fuck that, Terri said we're going to find out where in the hell this fag lives and we're going to take his shit there. Did you get a plate on that Mercedes, she asked? You know I did I said I already called Jeff on his shift and had it ran. Jeffrey Cammons was my ex who was also a police officer that hated Derrick's guts for breaking us up. Though that wasn't entirely the case, I had just as much to do with it as anyone. Did Jeff get the address for you, Terri asked? You know that Jeff was on it, I said but I'm not going over to a man's house to confront him about my man. The hell you not, Terri replied I will be there in five minutes flat…

CH. 1

JANICE...

Ring, Ring, Ring my doorbell chimed. I hesitated because I didn't want to deal with Terri and her dramatics but I was the one who called her with my problems. Coming I yelled as I went to answer the door, hurry your ass up Terri yelled back and stop procrastinating we are going to this fags house. I don't think that I'm strong enough to deal with this right now, I replied, heading back upstairs. Wait one got damned minute, she said, you woke me up out of bed on Saturday, my only rest day of the week, and now you want to back out? That won't work today sweetie get back down here and let's go right now. I came back downstairs, I'm ready I say. Ready for what Janice a PTA meeting, Terri asked? What's wrong with me, I asked? Everything, she answered; first of all why do you have on that church dress? Go you're behind right back up those stairs and put on something sexy, and where in the hell are Derricks things? I didn't know that we were taking his things with us, I replied. Why wouldn't we, she asked? I know you're not thinking about letting him come back here, she said. I'm not thinking about that Terri I Say, this is hard enough for me without you making it even more difficult. How in the world am I making it more difficult, she asked? I don't know how this is even possible Terri I said, how do you not know that the person that you are sleeping with on a daily basis is gay? Well, to be honest with you Terri answered I always felt that he had feminine ways the way he fusses over those thick nappy braids of his, and he spends more time in the mirror than you do, and he does have more skin care products than you, but gay, I can't honestly say that I saw that coming either. I thought about what she said and had to admit that Derrick did get those braids done every two weeks religiously. He did own more skin care products than I did, and all of his colognes had very soft scents as if they could be unisex. It doesn't matter though; I still couldn't see him being gay, I thought to myself, as I headed back up the stairs to change. I thought about his flawless light brown skin and his soft body, also how striking his features are and those full round lips. Honestly I can see men being attracted to him, he's gorgeous. People have actually said that we look a lot alike. I just passed it off as one of those things that they say about being with someone for a long time; sometimes they begin to resemble one another. I ran back upstairs to change clothes. I had no idea what she expected me to put on. What's proper attire for confronting your man and his gay lover anyway? What if I have HIV, I asked Terri as I returned from upstairs? I changed into my favorite jeans, the ones that hug all of my curves. I'm only five feet five but I'm really curvy. Terri and I both have beautiful caramel brown skin; the same hazel brown eyes full lips and perfect little button noses. People that haven't known us for a long period of time always think that we're related. I wear my hair really short and Terri wears hers long and straight down her back but ironically we both have the same texture. My life is on the line here, I said to her. I didn't even think about it like that she replied this is scary. I didn't pack his things yet either I said. I told her that I felt that I had to catch them together, before I confront him. She asked me was I crazy? This is nothing to be dragging your feet on, let's keep this short, simple and as low profile as possible, she said. I asked her to please trust me to deal with this my way because something inside just tells me that it's more to this than meets the eye. Terri said that although she hated that idea she would let me handle it my way. We got in her car and decided to go over to the address that I had obtained from Jeffrey and take a look around. The neighborhood was very upscale and wreaked of money. There was beautiful condo's everywhere. I pointed out the one that we were searching for. The same Mercedes that I had saw the night before, was sitting out front. We sat there for about twenty minutes trying to figure out what to do, when suddenly the door opened. There he was, the guy that I had witnessed Derrick kissing in the mouth the night before. Much to our surprise, instead of Derrick, there was a rather attractive young lady around my age on his arm. The lady was a little taller than I around Derrick's complexion or maybe a little lighter but she was gorgeous. What is going on here, I asked Terri? How am I supposed to know, Terri answered? It looks to me as if both of these fags have women at home. Hearing Terri refer to Derrick as a fag, kind of got to me. I feel she can take things too far too fast sometimes. I guess she picked up on my vibe because she looked right at me and said; I know you not getting an attitude because I called that fag a fag. I told her that I wasn't getting an attitude about anything but that she was putting the cart before the horse as usual. How am I putting the cart before the horse and you saw the sissy kissing another man in the mouth, she asked? What is it going to take to wake you up Janice, she added? I'm not sleeping on this I replied, not at all. I told her that it was just a hard pill for me to swallow. Where in the hell is Derrick if he's not here, I said more thinking out loud than asking. I have no idea sweetie, she answered but I do know that I'm hungry. Let's go think this out over breakfast she said driving off, I'm buying. We went down to the local IHOP where Terri greedily gobbled down as many pancakes and sausage as she could and washed it all down with a whole carafe of O.J. For the life of me, I don't see how she keeps her great shape the way that she eats. Terri's only about three or four inches taller than I am. I know that I have a banging body but compared to her perfect c-cups, size twenty four waist and hips and behind, I'm virtually invisible. She has the perfect husband. She got the total package the first time around, right out of college. How lucky is that? Todd was about six feet tall, dark and extremely handsome. He was the best husband and father that any woman could ask for; he was also the best friend that you could ever have. Todd was the kind of person that would give you the shirt right off of his back and I mean that literally. I wasn't very hungry after all my whole life had gone to hell overnight. I never understood that saying; what a difference a day makes, the way that I understand it now. I can't eat, I have no appetite Terri I say, please take me home, I have the worst migraine in the world. We got back to my house and Derrick's car still wasn't there. Derrick probably took his trifling behind home with somebody else's man, Terri said. Do you really think that he has multiple partners, I asked? Who knows she said looking just as confused as I felt. Do you want to come over to my house for a while and get some rest, Terri asked? I declined and told her that I was going in the house to try and get some sleep before Derrick showed up. Why do you tolerate him spending nights out anyway, she asked me at the same time easing in the fact that I could do much better. We don't have to worry about that anymore Terri I said, remember that I saw him kissing another man last night. I told her that I would call her and let her know everything, as I got out of the car. I went into my empty house, walked into the kitchen got a glass of water and two of my migraine pills. I swallowed them, undressed, climbed into bed and dozed off. I don't know how long I had been sleeping when I heard the door slam. Finally he was here. What do I do? What do I say? God was I nervous....

CH. 2

JANICE...

Terri and I grew up together from toddlers; our parents were best friends. Once they even fell out of friendship about my mom bad mouthing Terri's dad. I don't know the exact story but rumor has it that Terri's mom was dating the guy and that he was a real player by reputation. According to rumor everybody was trying to warn her about this guy, even my mom. Eventually they ended up not speaking to each other over him. One night during their little spat, my mom supposedly ran into Curtis (that's Terri's dad's name) in the local bar that they both visited pretty frequently. Curtis approached my mom, whose name is Latonya but everyone calls her Tiny Baby, which may have been an appropriate nick name for her then at size five-six, but right now at sixteen-eighteen isn't working out. This guy Curtis was a real dog because he knew that mom and Niecy which is Terri's mom's nickname but her real name is Faniece and she hates it. Well as I was saying, he knew that they were best friends. I guess he was trying to get with my mom by telling her that that he and Niecy had broken up. He decided that since the two of them weren't speaking that he would play both of them against each other. My mom was single at the time so he told her that Niecy was not her friend and that she never was. He said that she always spoke of mom as a jealous female that was bitter at her because of his and Niecy's relationship, being that she seemed unable to keep one of her own. Curtis had also said that the reason for him and Niecy's breakup was that he had found out that she slept around a lot, even though the two of them hadn't spoken in about six months, my mom said that she saw right through him. She knew that he was trying to convince her to get even with Niecy by sleeping with him. They said that my mom didn't fall for it though and that she and Curtis had gotten into a heated argument that night. I guess that when mom decided to go away to college she felt that it was time to clear the air with her best friend, plus she missed her more than words could say. She finally caught up with Niecy and was shocked to see that she was pregnant. They apologized to each other and begin to catch up on everything that they had missed out on in each others life. My mom asked Niecy who was the father of her child and was surprised to find out that it was the infamous Curtis Hampton and that they had never broken up after all. Niecy began to cry and told mom how she had been right all along about him and that he was really a dog. Mom said that she just sat there in total shock and at a lost for words, listening to her talk about all the terrible things that she had been going through with Curtis. Niecy went on and on about how things had gotten worse during her pregnancy and how many women she had caught him with. She told mom that she had expected that he had been seeing someone from her side of town and asked her if she knew anything about it. Mom said that she had seen him over at the bar a few times. I figured you did girl she said. Mom asked her what she meant by that. I just figured that you probably saw him with someone because he came in one night and couldn't stop talking about you. What could he have possibly told you about me mom asked? It's not even important anymore girl, Niecy replied, all that matters to me right now is that I got my friend back in my life and never again will I allow any person, place or thing to come between us. Mom could no longer control her tears and neither could Niecy they cried and hugged each other for about twenty minutes off and on. Well like I said that's what the rumor was around town and when Terri and I asked that's what we were told, but we didn't care about the details. We just vowed to never let a man come between us and to always be there for each other. We both grew up together on the east side of Detroit; we always attended the same public schools. My mom was an attorney and Terri's mom was a marketing executive for a fortune five-hundred company. Our moms were closer than sisters Terri is several months older than I am. Neither of us had ever been to daycare, our moms worked together when it came to us. My mom had always baby sat for Niecy and Niecy had always done the same when it came to me. We both had attended the same college. I majored in criminal justice and eventually became a high profile attorney, following right in moms footsteps. It's not like I had any other footsteps to follow in being that I never knew my dad. My mom was raped coming home from a party the year that she went away for college and I'm the product of that. Terri on the other hand majored in computer technology and is now an instructor at one of the top universities here; of course we know that her father is the infamous Curtis. That's as far as her mom would ever go on that subject with her. Therefore we were both raised by single mothers that never had anymore children, though they're both married now to wonderful men. That's another thing that we have in common Terri and I, we both love and adore our stepfathers. My stepfather's name is Randy Nelson and my mom married him fresh out of college. He's a foreman at a well known automotive company here in Detroit. Terri's stepfather Norman is an attorney so he and my mom not only get along great but bores the heck out of Terri's mom and my step dad, when they get together and start comparing job related issues. They usually dominate all the conversations. I have no children because for some reason I can't seem to stay in a stable relationship. I don't know what's wrong with me. I think that I'm just a loser magnet. I don't know why, but it seems that men are always hurting me. First there was Timothy whom I dated in college. The relationship was wishy washy right from the start, for one he was way more experienced. I wasn't a virgin; it's just that I had very little experience, so to me he was great in bed. I suppose all of his experience and my lack of caused him to venture out to more exciting activities on campus, also known as more experienced women. One thing led to another and I ended up sleeping with one of my professors and realized that Tim wasn't the best thing since sliced bread after all. One day Terri and I decided to catch a matinee at the local theatre near the campus. There we ran right smack into Timothy and his after school project that he had told me earlier he would be working on all night. I immediately wanted to walk away as if I didn't see them to avoid an incident. Terri took control as usual with her take no stuff attitude. She stepped right up to his face and let him have it. She's always been overprotective of me that way. I guess that's why I love her so much and I don't know what I would do without her. The thing with the professor and I didn't work out either, his wife and kids of course played a big part in that. That's why this relationship with Derrick meant so much to me. I have put my heart and soul into it. I just can't imagine Derrick being involved with a man. I'm not a fool. I know that he's not faithful. I knew that he messed around a little here and there, but nothing serious. I figured he was smart enough and cared enough not to jeopardize our relationship. How could I have been so wrong?

CH. 3

TERRI...

I love Janice with all my heart; I swear I do, but she is the most naïve gullible person in the world. She would let a fucking rattle snake convince her that he was a damn reindeer. There's not a better attorney in our city than she is, but the losers that she allows into her life is baffling to me. We've been best friends since diapers I guess; our parents are best friends also. We grew up closer than sisters; both of our mothers were single parents for a while. They don't have siblings either so they looked out for one another. We never had to endure daycare Janice and I because they pitched in and helped each other out in any way that they could. There was a rumor about them not being friends for almost a year. According to rumor Mrs. Latonya that's Janice moms name but we call her Tiny Baby. She had tried to warn my mom that my deadbeat dad was no good for her. My mom, who's just as clueless a Janice, when it comes to men, got angry and stopped speaking to her best friend. It wasn't until some time later after he had gotten my mom pregnant and ran around on her, with every tramp in the city of Detroit that she came to her senses. Mrs. Latonya had decided to go off to college but really needed to have her best friend back in her life, so she went and found mom. She found her all messed up pregnant by that dog of a father of mine, heartbroken and disgusted. They ended up back friends thank God because I don't know what I would do without Mrs. Latonya in my life. I don't even want to think about where in the world Janice would be without me to look after her either. Mrs. Latonya had Janice several months after I was born while she was away in college. Her father was never spoken of. I think that maybe she was raped or something before she went off to college. My mom told me that she had never saw Mrs. Latonya with a man before college so when she gave birth several months after her she was shocked. Mom also said that Mrs. Latonya refused to ever say anything about Janice's father. Mom also said that she would look very sad and distraught every time the conversation came up, so mom stopped asking. Mom told me that Curtis went on a trip right before I was born and that she had never heard anything from him again. According to her, she didn't want to either, ever. Therefore I never met Curtis and wouldn't want to if I could; after all I have the best dad that anyone could ever ask for. Back to Janice I bet you a million dollars that she is not going to confront that faggot Derrick head on. I know Janice she will beat around the bush at most. I wouldn't even be surprised if she doesn't say anything at all. I saw that pitiful look on her face when I referred to him as a fag. She had the nerve to talk about me putting the cart before the horse. Who says lame lines like that anymore? She can talk all of that putting the cart before the horse mess if she wants to, but that's not going to change the fact that Derrick's getting the hell out. Why can't he go live with his rich boy friend, who cares as long as he's out of Janice's life? I have tried every trick in the book to get rid of him, but Janice has fought me on it tooth and nail. I eventually gave up because I realized that she really loved him. I'm married and I have a son named Brandon. My husband Todd and my son are the most important things in my life, but Janice is right up there in the same category with them in my heart. I will not stand around and let her be walked on by anyone. She still hasn't called me and its noon. I know Derrick came home sometime yesterday because if he hadn't, I would definitely have known that. All of a sudden now she decides that she wants to handle something herself. That's just her way of saying that she isn't going to do anything. I remember once in college she was dating this loser that was mooching off of her. Everyone on campus tried to warn her about him. One day when he was on one of his all night study ventures, we ran into him and some bimbo at the movies. The first thing that came out of Janice's mouth was let's turn around and leave. Can you believe that, turn around and leave. Well that didn't happen because I marched right up to that negroes face and let him have a piece of my mind. Janice was upset with me at first, but she got over it when she found that he was engaged to that female, and that everybody knew about it but her. Well I can't wait any longer for her to call me so I'm going to call her right now.

CH. 4

DERRICK...

I came in today and Janice had this real messed up look on her face, like she had seen a ghost or something. I will never understand women if I live to be a hundred. They always seem to say one thing and mean another like you are supposed to read their mind or something. I should probably understand them perfectly me being the way that I am and all, but the truth is I'm clueless right now. It's funny how you search all your life for the one person that's put here on earth for you, and just when you think that you have it all figured out, destiny hits you right in the face. I got a good thing going here with Janice. I really love her; I just can't keep doing her this way. I don't want to leave her, but I don't see how I can stay. I will love her as long as I live, I swear. They say that honesty is the best policy, but that will never work in my case. Honesty will get me killed, that's what honesty will do for me so, what do I do? I will just keep pretending and doing what I do; hey if it isn't broke don't fix it, right? It would be if, I didn't love her so much, then she got this nosy ass best friend named Terri that I hate. Ain't no love lost though she hates me too? This broad thinks she's Janice's mama or something. She's always on my back; she can sniff out a lie like a bloodhound. It doesn't matter though they will never figure me out, hell sometimes I can't figure me out myself. I know that one day I'm going to have to come clean and make a choice, but today just isn't that day. I got a friend that knows exactly who and what I am and accepts it for what it is. We were just friends that could be honest with each other and talk about our problems at first. The next thing I knew things were all heated and complicated as hell. I got this ring for Janice because I knew that she was getting fed up with me. It's not an engagement ring though I wish it was but marriage takes honesty and like I said before; honesty in my case will probably end my life. I hear the room door open; here she comes with that look on her face. Here comes the drama I'm not ready for this shit.

CH. 5

JANICE...

I'm in total shock. Derrick came dragging his sorry behind in here last night, talking to me like I was a total idiot. You can't name an excuse that I haven't already heard from him, so now he's doing repeats. Last night was an old classic. He rode to Chicago with the boys. That with the boys shit has taken on a whole new meaning for him now, as far as I'm concerned. My best friend Terri and I spent most of our Saturday sitting outside of some rich gay guy's condo. I wanted so badly to see Derrick and his boy toy come out together so that I could confront them. I would have given anything to see the look on his face and to hear what he had to say for himself. That didn't happen though because instead of Derrick and the guy coming out, the guy came out with a rather attractive young lady. Terri thinks that both Derrick and the gay guy is a couple of down low brothers; you know guys that sleep with other guys secretly but portray the life of men. I really intended to let Derrick have it and throw him out of my house. I had taken a migraine pill and slept for a couple of hours, when I finally heard Derrick coming upstairs to the bedroom. I felt nervous, hurt, and confused all at the same time. He walked right up to me and kissed me on the mouth, usually this melts my heart, but today it makes me want to throw up. I dart for the bathroom and completely wash my entire face. Don't act like that sweetie, Derrick says. I want to say something but nothing comes out. Instead I just stand there, look at him and fight back the tears, as I wonder what happened to us. Why are you looking at me that way, he asked? What way is that, I said back to him, finally finding some words. You know exactly what I mean, he answered. Where have you been Derrick, I asked? Is that what you're upset about babe, he asked? I rode to Chicago with some friends of mine last night, we didn't decide to go until really late, so I didn't want to wake you up just to tell you that I wasn't coming home, he replied. I'm so tired of hearing these same old lies over and over Derrick, I say. Why do you even bother with this relationship, evidently this is not what you want so would you please... Before I could say the word leave Derrick yelled shut the fuck up with that dumb shit Janice, I don't want to hear it! I was stunned. Derrick has never yelled at me that way before, so I burst out into tears. Derrick turned and went down the hall to the den, good I needed to regain my composure. Finally I made up my mind to go right down the hall behind him and face him head on; there will be no more beating around the bush. I'm going to be just like Terri for once in my life and get some back bone. I closed my eyes for a moment, to collect my thoughts, let's see besides the fact that he's made a habit of spending nights out there's also the fact that we don't talk or spend any time together anymore. Then there's the grand finale of all; I saw Derrick kissing another man in the mouth with my own eyes. Even if he has an explanation for everything else, how in the hell does a man explain to his woman why he was kissing another man in the mouth? I opened my eyes and headed in the direction of the den when suddenly I felt dizzy as hell. Then it hit me that I had stopped taking my pills, Derrick doesn't know it though. Every time I start talking about having a family he acts as if he's allergic to the subject. I'm not waiting any longer, well I wasn't then but this is now, everything has changed. What if I am pregnant? That would be a disaster now wouldn't it? I can't deal with this shit at this moment, I say to myself as I turn around and head back for my bed. He deserves to sleep his ass in the den tonight; it will be the last night he spends in my house anyway. Right now all I need is some rest. I was awakened by the constant ringing of the phone. I know its Terri, I can feel it in my bones, plus that's the only time Derrick will let the phone ring a hundred times but he will not answer it. I'm not answering it either. I refuse to talk to her right now, God I wish I would have left her out of this. That's just nonsense though, Terri's all I have, she's just too damn nosy and aggressive sometimes, especially when it comes to me. I can't believe I slept all night either; my eyes are all puffy from crying. Once again I head in the direction of the den, this time I actually reach it and to my surprise Derrick is wide awake. We need to talk I say to him, we aren't doing anything but wasting each others time Derrick, something has to change, I say to him. You're right about that, he says. Something does have to change Janice, I've thought about this all night. Where do we go from here, I asked. I have only one suggestion, he says. What's that, I ask? I say we go to the alter, take the next step, and stick it out, most of all shut Terri's big ass mouth up. That's why I'm in shock standing here speechless looking at this expensive ass ring wondering when did he get it, and what kind of game was he playing. This is not going to solve our problems Derrick, I said. Why can't you give us a chance, he asked? Before last night this would have been like a dream come true for me, but right now this morning it's a nightmare, I replied. I'm not leaving you Janice, he said I've thought about this for a long time every since I realized how in love with you I am. How can you love me Derrick when you spend at least three nights a week out in the streets? That's going to end today Janice; he said. I won't be doing that anymore. from this day forward I will behave like a man that has a woman at home that he loves. Once again I'm blown away, at a lost for words why in the hell couldn't he have said all this before last night? I stood there like a fucking zombie and let him slide that ring on my finger knowing that none of this is real. Derrick is gay and according to rumor supposedly engaged to a very rich young man on the other side of town. I wanted to ask questions, but I didn't. I just sat there crying again looking stupid and to my surprise Derrick began to cry also. Derrick told me to get showered and dressed so that we could go out and celebrate. I went to my room to start getting ready, I wanted to make a fast exit; Terri would only be avoided so long. I was surprised that she hadn't bust up in here like the police already. I'm going to get some answers, just not from Derrick; he's not going to tell the truth. I'm going to conduct my own investigation and try to leave Terri out as much as possible, plus she's probably going to kick my ass when she sees this ring on my finger. I love Derrick and I really did want to stick this one out. I guess that's the real reason why I was trying to get pregnant and I probably would have been by now if he weren't so stingy with the dick. Everything makes more sense to me now. Derrick had been the one that insisted on us really getting to know each other before sex. It was all-cute to me at first but after three months, I was starting to believe that he wasn't physically attracted to me at all. That wasn't the case though and it was well worth waiting for, never before had a man been so attentive to my sexual needs. I swear it was as if he knew my body personally. I also found out that he was very shy about his body, and I don't know why because he's in great shape. Me myself, I have always been shy about being completely naked in front of someone. This was the first time that I had ever been with a guy that didn't try and pull the covers off of me to get a better view. That's why I really connected with Derrick; he didn't mind me undressing under the covers, because he did the same thing. I also love the fact that he never asked me to perform oral sex on him. Let's save something for marriage, he would always say. It's like I said, Derrick was well worth waiting for, he could make me feel better with basic sex than any other man could. I just don't understand how he would be attracted to another man; it's not fair to me. Why should I just step aside and let some fag take my man? I won't let it happen, but what do I do about it? I sat on the bed to think about it for a minute, then I felt his hand on my back, he began to kiss my neck, he pulled those covers over our heads. Like I said Derrick is great in bed second to none and we haven't even begun to explore our sexuality yet. I love Derrick and I know that he loves, me so what, he's made a few mistakes but I've managed to deal with them so far. Maybe he's not gay; maybe he was just experimenting with something and came to his senses, after all he didn't go home with that guy. Terri and I saw the gay guy coming out of his house, with that nice looking lady, maybe they both made a mistake. I know what I have to do; I have to go talk to Marvin's brother. That's what I will do; I will go to him and ask him what is really going on.

CH. 6

TERRI...

I knew it! I knew it! I knew damn well that Janice retarded ass didn't put that faggot bastard out of her house. I tried to call her all this morning and she didn't answer the phone, but I'm not stupid, I know when she's trying to avoid me. The first time I went over there neither one of their cars were there, so I figured they were somewhere together. I parked down the street behind an already parked car. They came pulling up about an hour later in Derrick's car. The way she was smiling when she got out of his car you would have never guessed that just forty-eight hours ago she had witnessed him kissing another man, in the mouth. I knew that his ass wouldn't hang around too long, he never does. She actually kissed him on the lips as she got out and ran into the house, like some little starry eyed school girl. After Derrick pulled off, I wasted no time pulling up in front of her place. Where is your car, I asked right off rip? Derrick followed me to the dealer, it's time for my oil change and annual inspection, she said. Now that you've mentioned it, why in the hell is Derrick still around, I asked? I asked you to let me handle this my way Terri, she replied and you promised. I know what I promised, I said but I know for a fact that I didn't promise to stand around and let my best friend get aids. Please don't say that Terri she whined, everything has changed in my life. I have to figure this out for myself. It's true, I said to her, everything has changed Janice, but you are making things worse by procrastinating. The quicker you let it go, the quicker you start healing. I think I'm pregnant Terri, she said. Please tell me that you are kidding, I say to her. No, I'm not kidding she said looking me straight in the eye, I may be pregnant she repeated as if I were deaf or really needed to hear it again. I know that you are not thinking about keeping it, I said to her, you are already at risk and now please don't tell me that you're entertaining the thought of bringing an innocent child into this catastrophe. How could you say something like that Terri, you know how long I've been trying to have a child of my own, she said. Wake the fuck up dum-dum, I shouted in her ear. I hate yelling at Janice but she acts like a five year old sometimes. How in the hell can she sit here and talk about having a baby with a man that's evidently involved with another man? I apologized to Janice for yelling at her. I know that she hates it when I do that. It's just that I love her so much and she can act so stupid at times. I have to admit that I lied when she mentioned HIV. Honestly that's all I could think about on the way to her house that morning. That's where I thought they more than likely were. I mean that's where I would have been because as soon as gay nuts would have come into my house, the conversation would have went just like this; I already know about you getting poked in the booty by that rich guy across town nigga, get your stuff out my house. Oh, wait but first follow me to the health department so that I can see if I got the heebie jeebies because if I do they can cancel your birthday for this year, and start putting your favorite pictures on the front of a T- shirt. I ain't lying. This is some serious shit. I don't know what to do, I'm nervous as hell but I can't be. I'm Terri, the strong one, well that's what I'm expected to be anyway. Fuck all that, what if she does have aids? What if she's pregnant and her child has aids? What the fuck do I do then? How did I let this happen? Where the hell was I? I've been so damn into myself lately, thinking only of my baby, my husband, and myself. What about my Janice, the only person that I have in the world besides my mom, step dad and Mrs. Latonya? This will definitely kill Mrs. Latonya Janice is her only child, that's why I can't believe that she's sitting here talking about having a baby with this person. Oh my God Janice, what are we going to do, I asked? I don't know Terri; she replied, the only thing that I know for sure is there's only one way that we are going to get any answers. What do you have in mind, I asked? I need to talk to that guy, Terri I really do, she said. What guy Janice, I asked? Marvin's brother, she said, the gay guy, Derrick's lover. What will you possibly say to him, I asked? I will know that when I get there Terri she said, all I know right now is that I need answers from him. All of a sudden a glare caught my eyes, oh God Janice please tell me that is not what I think that it is on your finger. It is Terri she said. She told me that she was waiting on the right moment to tell me that Derrick her and Derrick were engaged. I wanted to slap Janice so damn hard, what the fuck is she thinking? How did this happen Janice, I asked. She started telling me about how she couldn't face Derrick when he came in and him sleeping in the den all night, just as I was thinking that she wasn't a total idiot she told me that they ended up making love unprotected again. Finally I was fed up, I couldn't take it anymore and I told her so. I don't know what this man has done to you Janice I said, but it's evident that you have lost your mind and I can't help you anymore. She began to cry again; she looked so pitiful, I couldn't help but to comfort her. I don't blame you for turning your back on me she said, I don't know how I got in this mess, all I know is that it's my mess, and you need to go home to your family and let me get myself out of it. This is bullshit, she knew damn well that I would not turn my back on her, I would not take my ass home to my family and mind my own fucking business, she knew damn well that I wouldn't. I suppose that's why we are on our way to the car rental agency, if we're going to investigate Derrick and company, we have to be discreet right? We got the car, a beautiful burgundy Cadillac if we're going to cruise that neighborhood we should fit in. Janice called Derrick on his cell phone; he didn't answer of course and according to her he didn't have to work today. We don't have a plan Janice, I reminded her. I know Terri she replied, but I have to do this I really need a piece of mind. We didn't see Derrick or the other guy, but we did see something very interesting and that was Marvin, Janice was right he was gorgeous.

CH. 7

ANTHONY...

I know for a fact that Derrick spent the night at that woman's, I think her name is Janice or something. He doesn't know that I even know about her, my brother Marvin told me though. This is the worst situation that I've ever gotten myself into. The worst part about all of this is having my brother think that I'm gay. I'm not gay by a long shot. Marvin and I have always been close growing up, it's always been Marvin and Tony, we were always a team like Be Be and Ce Ce Winans, we just can't sing that's all. Marvin and I have been going at it for months, he couldn't wait to come running up in here night before last. I was just about to turn in, Derrick and I. when I answered the door and Marvin came rushing in. He had no idea that Derrick was in my room. Derrick always parks in the garage, I'm ok with it though, after all what would my neighbors think if they saw his car here all night? Anyway here comes Marvin telling me about some woman that he'd just met in the club, and was about to take home and screw according to him. He claims that he had gotten her all the way inside his car when suddenly Derrick pulled up. Marvin said that the woman got very nervous and told him that Derrick was her man. Derrick told me he was living with a roommate that he needed to come clean with before we go public. I can't see how in the hell he let his life get so complicated. We started off confiding in each other about issues at the job, we are both engineers at the same electronics company. Then all of a sudden things got heated for a moment, I thought I was beginning to have gay tendencies. Thank God that things aren't always what they seem to be. I have to admit that I really believed that the Janice lady was just a roommate. I knew the truth would come out sooner or later. The only problem now is how do I handle it? Do I come clean with Derrick and let him know that I know the truth about Janice, that I know she's not a roommate but a girlfriend? I don't think it will be a good idea, after all we are about to get married, I need to know if I can really trust Derrick. I'll just wait and see if he comes clean with me. I wish I could have been a fly on the wall over there though, I know that she tore into Derrick's behind. It's not everyday that you find out that the man that you've been with for over a year is not what you think that he is. I was expecting to hear all about it when Derrick showed up a couple of days later. Well it didn't happen; actually Derrick acted as if nothing happened at all, but how could that be? I have no idea what's going on right now but there's one thing that I do know, and that's this. I will not stand for much more of this. After all I don't remember asking to be put in the middle of this lie that Derrick is living. If nothing else, the most important thing to me, like I said before; is coming clean with my brother. Even though he's doing his best to accept me as he thinks I am, I can see the hurt in his eyes? Can you imagine finding out that after twenty-eight years of being as thick as thieves that your identical twin is gay? I think that the worst part of this for Marvin is not seeing it coming. God knows that we had our share of the honeys all through high school and college. I love my brother though and I can't stand hurting him like this, he's even trying to help me find the perfect time and place to tell mom and dad. Like I said he's trying but it's killing him and I can't wait to tell the truth. That's why he was so happy to come and tell me about the Janice lady. I told Marvin to leave it alone and to please let me handle it. I hope he listens…

CH. 8

JANICE...

I saw Marvin coming out of the condo right across the street from his brothers. I found out that the brother's name is Anthony but everyone calls him Tony, they are identical twins. They are twenty-eight years old, I'm thirty and Derrick's twenty-nine so we're all in the same age range. Terri and I had rented a car and rode through there trying to catch Derrick and Anthony together. Marvin stepped out to get something from his car, that I hadn't even noticed sitting out there. I asked Terri to pull over to him and let the window down, she did. I called out to him, at first he didn't have any idea who I was but then he seemed to relax. I could tell by the look on his face, that he knew why I was there. If you're looking for Anthony he's not home, he said. I asked him who was Anthony, and he said my brother, the one that's engaged to your boyfriend, that is why you're here isn't it? I saw no need to lie, so I came clean and told him the truth, that my whole life has been falling apart since I saw him last. Much to my surprise, Marvin looked rather confused himself. Would you like to come inside with me and talk for a while, he asked? I told him I didn't think that was a good idea. I promise that I won't bite you, he said sarcastically. How cute, I replied. It's just that I have so much on my mind right now. I feel that we should go inside and talk about it before you get into a head on with those two, he said. Terri thought that it was a great idea also. So she suggested that I go inside and talk with Marvin before we get caught out here playing detective. Finally I told Marvin that I would, but that he would later have to give me a ride to Terri's. He said that it wouldn't be a problem so Terri pulled off and we went inside. Once inside Marvin's condo, I felt as if I had died and gone to heaven. I thought I had a nice house but it couldn't hold a candle to this one. This place was beautiful; he had better taste than the average woman. This place should have been featured in Better Homes and Gardens, or at least MTV CRIBS. Would you like a drink, Marvin asked. Sure what do you have, I asked? Name your poison; he shot back looking more handsome than I remembered. Marvin made us two double shots of cognac on ice, and for the first time since I walked through his door, I began to relax. I know Terri, she has a hidden agenda in all of this. I know that the reason she agreed to go through with this at first is because she would never let me go through something like this alone. Still she showed no enthusiasm at all until we saw Marvin coming out of that door. Terri's eyes lit up like a light bulb had gone off inside of her head. I hope she doesn't have any match making ideas. Each and every time I try my hand at love I fail miserably, I just want to get this over with. Finally Marvin broke the ice, asking me how long had Derrick and I been together. I told him that we had been together for over a year. How long has he been seeing Anthony, I asked? Marvin told me that Derrick and Anthony had been seeing each other for about six months as far as he knew. He told me that at first he thought nothing of it, because it just seemed as if they were two work buddies that had taken to hanging out with each other. When did you notice that it was more than that, I asked? He answered and told me that he had noticed that it was more to it a couple of months back when he had witnessed the two of them kissing. According to Marvin he was expecting the arrival of a female friend of his, a booty call no doubt, late one night. He said that he had heard a car outside, and thinking that it could be her went to take a peek out of the window. He said that he saw Derrick letting Anthony out of his car. He said that he thought nothing of it until Derrick got out of the car and proceeded to walk Anthony to the door. All of a sudden Marvin held his head down at first and then looked up at me and said; then they started kissing. I felt so sorry for Marvin at that moment he looked like he had lost his best friend, I guess in a way he had. I never had a brother and Terri is the closest thing that I have to a sister, but if I woke up tomorrow and found out that she was gay, I don't know how I would take it. We talked a little about our families and our backgrounds, I was really impressed at how much we had in common, and how easy he was to talk to. Much to my surprise, I found out that Anthony doesn't have a girlfriend at all like Janice and I thought. Marvin said that he had seen him with the same woman that we seen him leaving with the other morning quite a few times lately. He said that it was totally shocking to him, especially after he had confronted Anthony the next morning about witnessing him and Derrick kissing on the doorstep the night before. According to Marvin, Anthony had admitted to him that he had fallen madly in love with Derrick, they were engaged to be married, he went on to say. According to Anthony the only thing they were waiting on was for him to find a way to tell his parent's, and for Derrick to find a way to tell his roommate. I'm sure that you can imagine how surprised I was to find out that I was just a roommate. My mind began to wonder all over the place. I started to think about all the lies, and all of the deceit. Finally I got the strength to speak again. Do you think that they are practicing safe sex, I asked? I try not to think about that, said Marvin but to be honest, I don't know. I'm going to take a HIV test anyway, I replied not knowing what else to say. I'm so sorry Janice, he said. You didn't do anything to be sorry about, I replied. I wonder if the woman that Anthony is seeing knows that he's bi-sexual, Marvin asked. I know damn well you're not asking me, I replied I was totally in the dark until the other night, remember? What's her name, I asked Marvin? What's whose name, Marvin asked? This woman that Anthony is seeing what's her name, I asked? I don't know, Marvin answered actually I've never been formally introduced to her. Don't you find that peculiar, I asked? I did at first, he answered, I even caught them coming out one day and tried to introduce myself. What happened, I asked? Nothing, he answered, Anthony rushed me off so damned fast I didn't know what to think. Maybe she's married or something, I said more thinking out loud than asking a question. Who knows, Marvin replied. All of a sudden I noticed that he was sitting rather close and that the cognac was kicking in. At that very moment I began to cry.

Marvin put his arms around me to comfort me and somehow or another our lips seemed to find each others.

CH. 9

TERRI...

Janice hasn't called yet; I hope that's a good sign. That Marvin guy is a real sight for sore eyes. I'm happily married and have never entertained the thought of cheating on Todd. Damn Derrick and everything that comes with his ugly black ass, is what I would have been thinking that night if I had met Marvin at that club. As good as he looks he could have been telling me that Derrick was a serial killer and all I would have heard was blah, blah and fucking blah. She's really suffering though, and I hope that she gets the answers she's looking for. I try not to let on to her how much this shit is scaring me and I'm not easy to scare. I stand to lose so much here, I don't know what to do, so I do what any red blooded American woman would do. I called my mother. All of a sudden I lost control of all my emotions, in tears I just let everything come out. My mom didn't say anything; at first I thought we had been disconnected somehow. Finally she spoke and said that I was going to have to pull myself together. She said that Janice was going to need me now more than ever, especially if she happens to be pregnant. I told her that I didn't know if I could be as strong as everyone expects me to be, after all I'm human too, Right? That eerie silence is in the air again, and I begin to sense that there is something else going on here. Are you still there mom, I ask? I'm here Terri, she answered as if she was thinking of something to say. Is everything all right mom, I asked wondering what in the world was going on with her. I suppose so Terri, she answered. What do you mean, you suppose so mom, I asked? My mom had never been one to have a loss for words ever, so I was getting scared as hell. I asked her to please tell me what was going on. Are you ok, is something wrong with dad, I continued. There goes that damn silence again. I just waited it out this time, and finally she spoke. I'm going to call Tiny, she said. Where in the world did that come from, I thought to myself. Then it hit me that she was going to tell Tiny about Janice's situation. Mom please you can't, I yelled! I can't what mom asked, sounding confused? You can't tell Tiny about Janice's situation it wouldn't be right she doesn't even know that I'm telling you, I said. I just didn't know what else to do but call you, I told her. Mom told me that I was right to call her but assured me that telling Tiny Janice's situation wasn't why she was calling her. Well if that wasn't the reason that you needed to call Mrs. Tiny so suddenly, then what was it I asked? As bad as the timing is right now she said, that there was something that Tiny and I have to tell the two of you. Mom you're scaring me, I said. There's no reason to be frightened, she said this is something that had to be done sooner or later. What has to be done ma, I asked frantically? Just get your sister and get over here as soon as you can Terri ok, she said. I think it's cute that sometimes mom refers to Janice and me as sisters; sometimes we even forget that we're not. They, whoever in the hell they are; say everything in life happens for a reason; damn how right they were.

CH. 10

JANICE...

I've really been stressed out these last few days, plus I haven't drank cognac in a long time either. Those are just a few of the excuses I was making up for myself to justify what had just happened. First I'm crying my eyes out on Marvin's shoulder and the next thing I know he's carrying me to his bedroom. Why didn't I stop it at the kissing part? Why didn't I want to? I thought Derrick's lovemaking was phenomenal, but Marvin made me realize that it was just different that's all. I feel like a terrible person; after all I do have Derrick's ring on. Marvin noticed that also. What are we going to do Janice; he asked looking me straight in my eyes. Before I could answer him my cell phone rang. Terri had rescued me once again, from what though at this moment, I have no clue. Why do I do these things to myself? Before I can solve one dilemma, I've gone and created another. Anyway Terri told me that she had called and told her mom all about this nightmare that I'm going through with Derrick. She apologized but I told her that it was ok; after all it was only a matter of time before I told her myself. We were just a close knit family like that. Then she told me that the reason she had called me was that her mom had called a family meeting right away and that she was on her way to pick me up as we speak. I couldn't help but wonder what the meeting would be about. Janice told me that Mrs. Faniece agreed to let me be the one to tell my mom, so what in the hell were we meeting about? I hurried into the shower, and Janice was there to pick me up almost before I could fully dress. Before leaving I turned to Marvin and asked how many nights does Derrick spend over at Anthony's during the week? Funny you should ask that, said Marvin but the truth is that he doesn't. What do you mean he doesn't, I asked? He never spends the entire night; Marvin went on to say that he had witnessed Derrick parking his car in Anthony's garage sometimes two or three nights a week. He's always gone by morning though I think Mrs. Married comes over wee hours of the morning. I always see her leaving in the morning, Marvin added. I wonder if that's what happened the other morning when Terri and I were watching to see if Derrick stayed the night with your brother. I'm sure that's what happened, Marvin answered but if you're talking about the night we met, Derrick's car wouldn't have been here anyway. Where was his car, I asked? He got drunk and left it at the club they rode in together that night, so Anthony must have drove him to it later on. That's some sex drive that your brother has, I replied, he's dropping off his man and picking up his woman on the way back home. That is kind of fucked up, Marvin replied with that same sad expression from earlier returning to his face. I walked over and gave him a hug and a quick kiss, Terri was blowing the horn. I will call you I said as I exited. I turned and looked in the direction of Anthony's condo, as I climbed in the car. I could have sworn that I saw Anthony's curtain move; maybe it was just my imagination. Terri asked me if i had seen Derrick or did anything happen? I told her no, but that Marvin and I had a good time talking. I saw a little smile on her face? What's that smile for, I asked? What smile she asked, trying to act as if she didn't know what I was talking about. The one that's plastered all over your face, I replied. I leaned back and relaxed for the first time since all this begin, it really didn't matter to me what happened. What do you think this is all about Terri, I asked? I have no idea, she replied but it sounds serious. It sure does, I said I'm really scared. I could tell that she was scared also, though she tried to hide it. I changed the subject and asked her what had my nephew been doing? She answered me back that he was being bad as hell. What was he doing when you left, I asked? Playing with his dad, she answered. Terri was the luckiest woman in the world to me, and I was happy for her, happy that she was my best friend, if I had a sister I would want her to be just like Terri. Little did I know how those words would come back to bite me in my ass? I will forever think of this day as the first day of the rest of my life.

CH.11

ANTHONY...

I just happened to be looking out of my window when I see this strange woman leaving my Brother Marvin's condo. Was it just my imagination or was she staring at my window? I've never seen this one before but she was a real looker, it doesn't matter to Marvin though because he's never taken any woman serious. They come and go with him. I was the same way until I met Derrick, so I'm not trying to judge him or put him down or anything of that nature. I feel so distant from my brother right now. I can't take this shit anymore; I have to come clean with Marvin. I just don't know where to start, this whole situation is like a nightmare, the only thing about this nightmare is waking up out of it, is going to be much more fucked up than anything, especially for this Janice lady. I kind of feel sorry for her, even though I don't know or have never seen or met her. I don't know why women these days don't seem to take out time to really get to know the men that they get involved with anymore. I've been through so many; I lost count a long time ago. I've played so many games and have caused so many women to shed tears that it's not even funny. The worst thing about that is why they're all emotional over me, I'm feeling like I don't even know them well enough for them to be acting like that. I'm not trying to low rate women but they should get to know a little bit more about who they are with before they start sleeping with them, that's all I'm trying to say. I hope that Derrick calls soon, I need some answers to a lot of questions that only he can supply. He has got to come clean with that woman regardless of what happens between the two of us, I just hope that she doesn't snap and kill his ass, because I don't know what I would do if I were in her situation. She might need therapy after this shit hits the fan, I know that I would. Well like I said, blood is thicker than mud, so no matter what Derrick decides to do I can't take hurting my brother anymore, and I would die and go to hell twice before I go to my mom and pops with some I'm gay shit. My mom is very dramatized as it is. I can see her fainting immediately. My dad though that's a totally different ballgame, that nigga will break his foot so far off in my ass, that they would have to amputate him from knee down. That's the reason Marvin keeps talking about waiting on the right time to break the news to them. He knows damn well that there isn't a right time. He's just trying to save me an ass kicking, for as long as he can. That's just my brother being my brother. He's always been there for me like that. That's all the more reason that I can't keep hurting him like this. If Derrick doesn't come clean with me about this woman I have no choice but to rethink spending the rest of my life with him. I feel that if he can live an almost two year lie with this Janice woman, what will be different about us? That's a good question huh? Ain't that a bitch while I'm sitting here wondering how other hoes get emotionally involved with these men before they really know who they are, looks like I need to take my own advice doesn't it? This is some complicated shit. I think I'll have a stiff drink and head on over to Marvin's. I'm still curious about who that hot chick was that he was letting out of his door, not only was she a looker, but so was the chick who's car she got in. I've got to find out who they are and get in on the action; after all I'm not married yet, right?

CH.12

TERRI...

When I picked Janice up from Marvin's house she looked more confused than she did when I dropped her off. She didn't talk much and I decided not to pry. I went home to some real shocking shit myself today. I won't even dare try and address it right now with all that's going on with Janice. The best thing to do is to deal with this bullshit with Derrick plus whatever in the hell is going on with my mom. I felt a panic go through me as I pulled into the driveway. I could tell that Janice was nervous as hell, that girl can't hide shit, her face talks louder than she does, in a game of poker you can clean house on her ass. I could see that Mrs. Latonya had beaten us here. My step dad's car wasn't here though; I guess the men wanted no part of this one, whatever it was. My mom opened up the door looking nervous as hell, this must be some serious shit, I started thinking to myself. I hope her old ass is not about to say she's pregnant or no stupid shit like that, because like I said before she is just like Janice when it comes to life matters, as clueless as hell. What did you cook mom, I'm as hungry as a hostage I said trying to break the ice. She answered that she had cooked some collard greens with smoked turkey wings, homemade macaroni and cheese, candied yams and cornbread so I headed straight for the kitchen with Janice right on my heels. What do you think this is about Janice asked me as we started piling food on our plates? I don't have the slightest idea, I replied. I got here at the same time you did remember, I joked. She laughed for the first time in days, she laughed, I mean she actually raised the corners of her mouth and laughed. That to me was worth a million bucks at this moment. I got to thinking that maybe leaving her there at old Marvin's house wasn't such a bad idea after all. Once again I would never know the punch that would pack until much later down the line. Once we were done piling enough food on our plates to feed a couple of ponies, we proceeded into the living room where our moms were waiting patiently for us. I sat on the love seat across from the sofa that both of our parents occupied and Janice sat on the floor beside me. My mom started to speak first. I know that you both are wondering what this is all about, she stated. Of course we are what kind of stupid question is that, I thought to myself. I really don't know where to start, she continued to say. The beginnings always a good place, I replied. Well the beginning is hindsight in this case smartass, she answered. We all laughed at her witty remark. Suddenly my mom got that serious look on her face again. Please mom tell me what's getting to you like this, I asked? Everything was quiet for a moment then Mrs. Latonya spoke up and said that she had recently found out that she had diabetes. She continued to say that one of her kidneys had failed and that the other one was barely functioning. Janice immediately broke into tears, and I followed right behind her. The two of you has got to hold it together, said my mom, trying to choke back her own tears. Mom exactly what does this mean, asked Janice? It means that I'm going to start dialysis treatments soon, she answered. What exactly does that consist of, I asked. Well she continued, once my other kidney finally fails I will no longer be able to urinate naturally, so they will have to filter my urine by machine, Janice looked horrified! It's really not as bad as it sounds, Mrs. Latonya went on to say, that they just hook you up to this machine and it filters the urine out of your blood by running it through these tubes. There is an alternative, my mom chimed in. What is that ma, I asked? A kidney transplant, she answered that's why we called this meeting. How long have you known this ma, asked Janice? Not very long at all, she answered. That's not the only matter at hand here Janice, Mrs. Latonya said. There's more, once again my ma cut into the conversation. What is it ma, I asked? We all must be tested immediately, she answered the quicker we find a match the better. That's the reason we decided that now was the time to tell the two of you what we are about to tell you, my mom said looking into space. She asked not to be interrupted until she was done speaking and she wasn't, but what she said would forever change our lives, Janice's and mines that is.

CH.13

JANICE....

Terri and I rode home practically speechless. Remember when I said that today would forever be considered as the first day of the rest of my life? Try finding out that your man is gay, your mom is dying if she doesn't get a kidney transplant, oh and let's not forget the show stopper, I have a sister all in a matter of days. I can't believe that after all these years finding out now at this point in my life that Terri is really my sister. I don't know if I can handle all of this at one time. Who said that God doesn't put more on you than you can bear? I personally think that they should take a peek into my life. Yep that was the grand finale of the great family meeting. Come to find out that all those years ago at the bar, old Curtis didn't crap out after all. That was what my mom really went to tell her best friend, when she found her pregnant, that she had been seeing Curtis secretly behind her back. Seeing that Mrs. Niecy was having his child and was still his girlfriend changed her mind. I guess that would have changed my mind too if I had been sleeping with a man that had slept with my best friend, I said to my mom rather harshly. Much to my surprise Mrs. Niecy damn near bit my head off. She grabbed me by my collar before I knew it and jacked my ass up. Then looking me dead in the eye as if she would tear my head off and believe me at that moment, there was no doubt in my mind that she would. She told me that if I ever spoke to my mother that way ever again she would kick my narrow ass, until it caught fire. That's the best friend I have in this world she said, more of a sister than if we were blood, and as long as I have breath in my body, no one will speak to her that way, especially you, she said to me. Curtis didn't give a fuck about neither one of us, she continued to say, she told me the truth the day Terri was born. She didn't find out till later that the bum had gotten her pregnant also. It didn't matter to me anymore at the time; the only thing that mattered is that I had my best friend back. I told that son of a bitch, to get the fuck out of my life and never come back, and I meant it. They both agreed to tell us when they thought that the time was right and what better time than now? That's the reason Terri and I rode home in total silence. Finally when we arrived at my place I reached over and gave her a hug. I always had this obsession with protecting you, she said speaking very softly I guess this explains it huh? You have always been my sister in my heart Terri, I replied. I know, she said. What are we going to do, I asked? We're going to go get tested for your mom, she said. I know that, I said but what are we going to do about this Derrick situation? Janice I will call you tomorrow, Terri said abruptly almost as if she was upset with me or something. I didn't understand her change in attitude at all; she didn't even wait until I got inside before she drove off.

CH.14

TERRI...

There are times when I want to knock the shit out of Janice and then there are times when I can just choke the life out of her silly ass. I love Janice with all my heart even before I found out that she was my sister. She just does and says the dumbest shit at the dumbest times. For example we had just found out that her mother could die of kidney failure due to diabetes right before finding out that my dad fathered the both of us. What does she do? Her simple minded ass chooses this moment to get judgemental and sarcastic towards her mom, damn near causing my mom, to break a foot off in her ass. Shit like that is what I mean by times that I can knock the shit out of her. I mean evidently they been got past that bullshit, they are still best friends so who in the hell are we to judge? The only reason that they chose to tell us in the first place is because of Mrs. Latonya's condition and she felt like if the worse happens we would know. I mean who really gives a fuck about what the hell happened way back when? They got over it so fuck what anybody else thinks about it. I can't believe Janice could have the nerve to say some smart ass shit to Mrs. Latonya, but she has yet to confront Derrick's faggot ass. Then as if that wasn't enough, just as I had got my mind off of the bullshit that she pulled on her mother, she asked me what we were going to do right? Of course I'm thinking that she's talking about her mom's condition, nope! That's just asking a little too much of Janice, this bitch actually had the nerve to say about Derrick. Can you believe that? I can't. These are the times that I would like to choke the life out of her, my God how can we really be related? I guess there's no wonder that I found another woman's phone number in my husband's pants pockets. I'm Terri though; you know the strong one, the one with all the answers and the one that everyone else turns to. There's only one thing wrong with this picture and that's this. Who the hell do I turn to? Isn't it funny that you can always see through everybody else's bullshit, but you can't see your own shit coming? I know one thing though and that's this; I ain't no Janice by a long shot I'm not tolerating no cheating from his ass. I've never cheated on him or even thought about it for that matter. We had always agreed that we would talk about things no matter how bad they were. So why is he accepting some woman's phone number, who the hell is she? Where did he meet her? When did this all begin? How far has it gotten? The biggest question of all is what am I going to do about it and where will it leave my son and me? All this shit that I've got to deal with and the only thing that Janice can think about is what are we going to do about Derrick. I guess now you can see why I'm so frustrated with her. How in the hell can she be thinking about a fag after spending the evening with that fine ass Marvin, anyway that's what I want to know? I'm not stupid though, I noticed that she had this peculiar look on her face when I picked her up this afternoon. I was so preoccupied with the family emergency meeting that I forgot to ask how it went. I'm almost scared to find out knowing Janice, nothing interesting probably happened anyway. Janice can fuck up anything no matter what it is. If you ask me she fucked up from the beginning with Marvin anyway. Why did Derrick have to pull his deadbeat ass up at that very moment? Why did she even care? She should have just ignored him pulling up and told Marvin to drive off as fast as he could. That wouldn't have worked though. Derrick would have seen her car in the parking lot, well maybe not. I feel that she should have taken a chance though; after all she did sit there long enough to witness him waiting on another man and greeting him with a passionate kiss. He didn't notice her then, right? I think that sometimes I'm too hard on Janice. I just want her to for once in her life, just stand up for herself. I may be a bit of a hypocrite also. I'm always telling her how to run her life and fix her problems, but yet here I sit in my driveway avoiding going inside of my own house so that I don't have to face my own. Todd is home, I know this because I opened the garage and he was parked in my spot as usual, that's one of the little things that he does to annoy me, but I don't let it really get under my skin. I don't understand how woman make a big fuss over little things like the toilet seat, leaving the cap off the toothpaste, taking my parking space. I smiled at the thought; as much as it annoys me everything that he does is cute to me, I guess that's what real love is all about being cute and annoying at the same time. I looked in my rearview mirror stared myself straight in the eyes and said, look Terri stop this bullshit, get out of here, go in there and face this head on just like you do everyone else's problems.

CH. 15

MARVIN...

The problem with being a twin is that somehow someway, no matter how hard you try to avoid it, you always end up in the middle of your siblings mess. Well at least that's always been the way it was with my brother Anthony and myself. I just found out a couple of months or so that he is gay. It doesn't matter how many times I say that to myself over and over, it just doesn't ring right in my ears. My brother, my twin brother is gay. We have grown up closer than close, thicker than thieves all of our life and I never would have imagined in my wildest dreams that I would be faced with this one day. It all started when I witnessed him and some guy that he works with named Derrick kissing. Now don't get me wrong red flags had gone up in my head. My brother and I were always inseparable as toddlers, young children, teens and adults. We did everything together, as young children we were tough little boys. Whenever we got in trouble we would never tell which one of us actually did the bad deed, so we both would accept punishment together. As teens we both dated cheerleaders, sometimes the same ones. I know that it was scandalous of us but at times we would switch up on our girlfriends. The first time Anthony thought that he was in love. I was a little jealous. I'm the oldest by eight minutes. I guess that's the reason that I've always been able to talk Anthony into seeing things my way. One day he comes home talking about getting engaged to Karen this cheerleader that I tried to date on several occasions, but she always turned me down flat. Anthony and I have totally different personalities. I was always a womanizer; Anthony on the other hand was what you would call the sensitive type, so he always got the better choice of women. As I was saying I had tried to take Karen out several times but to no avail. I don't know when Anthony started dating her; actually I couldn't believe that anyone had even gotten to first base with her stuck up ass. Since we always shared everything with each other, I asked him how far he had gotten with her. Much to my surprise, I found out that he was hitting that on a regular basis. Well like I said at first I was a bit jealous, for one that she was taking up too much of my brother's time, and for two she never gave me the time of the day. I tried to talk some sense into him about this girl, but he wasn't hearing it. Then on the Fourth of July weekend my parents announced that they were going away to Myrtle Beach and since we had just turned seventeen we could stay home alone. as you can guess, to two seventeen year old boys with raging hormones that was just like saying Christmas came early this year. My parents left at about four thirty a.m. I had every intention on sleeping in late that morning, but to my surprise I was awakened by sexual sounds coming from Anthony's bedroom. I got out of bed and tipped down the hall. Anthony's door wasn't locked so I quietly turned the door knob. There was stuck up ass Karen riding Anthony like a porn star. Funny she didn't look so high and mighty now, but I must admit that she did look sexy as hell. I decided right there at that moment that I must have some of that. I don't know why parents always dress twins the same. I think that's one of the silliest things that people do. We already have the same face, which take away from our individuality from the moment that we are born, so whatever in the world would make you think that we want to be dressed alike on a daily basis also? I personally can't speak for all twins but it aggravated the hell out of Anthony and me. As soon as we were able to dress ourselves we stopped the twin dressing immediately, never the less, it didn't stop my mom from buying in twos. Well after being woke up early, and entertained by those two going at it, like I said, I made up my mind that I had to have me some of that. I went to the bathroom and had my shower, when I came out Karen was in my mom's kitchen cooking breakfast. I walked in, spoke, grabbed a plate and joined the two of them at the table; the girl could cook her behind off, and what a great behind it was from my view. Once the table was cleared Karen went upstairs to take her shower and get dressed. I had to move quickly at this point. I was born with asthma, a cloud that on this day would bear its silver lining. I grabbed my chest and began to fake an attack; Anthony reacted just as I knew he would and rushed over to my side. Where's your inhaler Marvin, he asked? I'm out, I replied going deeper into my make believe attack. Instantly Anthony grabbed his car keys and rushed out to the pharmacy. As soon as I heard the car start up I ran to my room and threw on my white tee and jeans, the exact twins to the ones Anthony was wearing at breakfast. Finally I heard the shower stop. That's when I sprang into action. I have to admit that I was afraid that she would see right through me, so I ran back to my bedroom and grabbed my blindfolds. I ran back down the hall and waited by the bathroom door. It seemed like forever before she stepped out into the hallway, I grabbed her from the back and kissed her on the neck, she giggled and tried to grab my hand, just then her towel dropped to the floor. What are you doing, she asked. Is that a trick question, I replied? What if you're brother catches us, she asked? Still holding her from back I walked her back into the bathroom, bent her over the sink and tied her eyes with blindfolds. Aren't you feeling pretty kinky early in the morning, she said assuming the position? I entered her from the back and damn did she feel good. As soon as we were finished I took the blindfold off and she turned around grabbed me by the neck and we kissed for what seemed like forever. Once we came up for air she started teasing me about getting her all dirty again and jumped back into the shower. I was just out of my clothes and hurrying back into my bathrobe when I heard Anthony's car pulling into the driveway. I ran downstairs to meet him, before he yelled my name out. I caught him just as he was coming in with my inhaler in hand. I found a half empty in the kitchen drawer; I said grabbing for the bag with the new inhaler in it. I ran all the fucking stop signs and red lights that I could get away with, he said, out of breath. Marvin why do you do dumb shit like this, he asked? I swear that my heart almost stopped at that question. How in the hell did he know? It wasn't entirely my fault; I lied feeling like shit still trying figure out how in the hell did he know that I just fucked his fiancé to be. Just before I opened my mouth and put my foot in it he yelled,

"You've had asthma since you were born nigga, you know damn well better than to run out of inhalers". I'm sorry, I said sweating like hell trying to regain my composure. Sorry my ass, you scared the hell out of me he said just as Karen came downstairs. I don't know why; call it guilt but for some reason I felt nervous as hell. I couldn't even look her in the face as she kissed Anthony on the cheek, waved good-bye to me, grabbed her car keys and said that she was running late for something or another. Sorry that I had to run out on you like that, Anthony said. Once again I froze in my tracks, but Karen either didn't hear him or was just in too big of a rush to pay attention to what he said because she just kept right on walking out the door. That was a close call I thought to myself as I headed back to my bedroom to finally get some sleep. Things got a little strange with us after that, because he no longer referred to Karen as his fiancé to be anymore. Much to my surprise he started to date other girls, lots of other girls, lots of my girls, so I dated his right back. It became a game to us and we kept it up into our college years, but there were never anymore talks of engagements or marriages. Why? I never knew, all I know is that I haven't yet met a girl that I could take that serious, as far as Anthony goes I don't know. Whatever Karen did to change his mind about getting engaged to her ass is probably what turned him into the womanizer that he became. Now that I think about it I never even saw much of her in school after that, eventually she disappeared altogether. I know I looked for her, because like I said before that was some good shit that she had between her legs, and regardless to what her and Anthony fell out about, he probably didn't want it anymore, but I sure did, but like I said, he never really spoke of her anymore, life went on and now he wants to marry a man, no matter how many times I say that out loud or in my mind it just doesn't ring right in my ears. I wish he would have gone ahead and got engaged and eventually married Karen's fine ass, shit at least maybe we wouldn't be facing this gay shit, and I could've pulled out my blindfolds and got some every now and then. Well there's one thing that I know for sure and that's this; he damn sure don't have to worry about us switching anymore because the way he's going now I just don't swing in that direction.

CH. 16

ANTHONY...

I knocked on Marvin's door about five times before he finally yelled out I'm coming! He opened the door in a bathrobe holding a glass of what looked like cognac in his hand. Can I get one of those, I asked as I went over to the sofa and sat down. Sure can, he answered, walking over to the bar. He handed me a double shot as I relaxed and got comfortable. What have you been up to, I asked? What you hear, Marvin joked back at me. I didn't hear anything I replied, but I saw a bad ass bitch leaving out of your door not long ago, and then I saw what appeared to be an even badder one, picking her up. You been holding out on your brother, I still got a little play left in me you know, I'm not hitched yet. It was an illusion, Marvin joked back. Since when did we start keeping chicks confidential, I asked as I noticed the serious look on his face? At that moment Marvin turned to face me and said, it's not fun anymore talking chicks with you and hell you running around with a dude, talking about marrying him and shit, it tears me up inside just thinking about it, and you think that I'm going to laugh and joke with you about it? Hell no. I know that I came over here to set the record straight with my brother, but who in the hell did he think he was talking to me like this? You can't choose who in the hell I fall in love with Marvin, I replied angrily. I never said that I could and I never tried to, he shot back. You know what Marvin, I yelled, I came over here to share some information with you that would ease your mind about my whole gay situation, but I just realized that I don't owe you an explanation, as a matter of fact, I don't owe you or anybody else shit. What about mom and dad, he shot back? What about mom and dad, I yelled mom and dad can't live my life for me or tell me how to live. I don't want to argue with you about this, Marvin replied. I just don't know how to handle this situation. You are my brother, my flesh and blood brother and for the life of me, I just can't see how I let this happen. What the fuck do you mean, how you let this happen Marvin, I yelled not so loud this time, it just kills you that you can't control this situation, it's my life not yours to control anyway, you are my brother not the fucking boss of me, I'm a grown fuckin man Marvin. I'm not trying to be the boss of you Anthony, he shot back; man it's just that I think that you are sick. What have I done to make you think that I'm sick, I asked? Fell in love, want to get married, have a meaningful relationship and maybe a couple of kids. Do you know how fucking twisted that shit you just said sounded Anthony, he asked? How in the hell do you suppose to have a meaningful relationship, marriage and fucking kids with another goddamn man. That's some sick shit, he repeated once again. I was so pissed off right now at this moment; I never wanted to get into a big falling out like this with my brother, but dammit we were here now and there was no turning back. Once again I began to speak, trying like hell to control my tone. Marvin as I said before you so rudely interrupted me; I came here to tell you something very important about Derrick's and my relationship that would probably ease your mind. Once again Marvin cut me off in mid conversation, I really can't stomach this shit right now Anthony another time bro, please another time. That did it. Shut the fuck up and listen to me Marvin, I yelled once again to no avail because he fuckin interrupted me again. I refuse to talk to you about this right now Anthony; he said, could you at least give me a couple of days and I promise that we can discuss this. I just turned around and left. I couldn't take it anymore. How in the hell can he judge me like this, calling me sick, like he's some kind of saint. I wanted to ease his mind, make everything all right. I love my brother and it's rare that we get into these arguments, but he really pissed me off today, I thought out loud to myself as I went back over to my place. I checked my machine as I made myself another double shot of cognac. Derrick had called. I can't wait to see his ass either, nobody's worth me getting into it with my brother like this I said to myself, nobody, as I began to undress and head for the shower.

CH. 17

DERRICK…

These last few months have been hell for me. I'm engaged to a woman named Janice that I live with. I'm also engaged to a man named Anthony across town. I don't know how Anthony found out that Janice was my girlfriend and not my roommate but shit it had to come out sooner or later right. I really love Janice but I don't know now at this moment. Anthony called me a few months ago tripping about me not telling him about Janice being my girlfriend and so on. He started talking about how all this is hurting his brother, and that they had this big fight about it. He wanted us to come clean, and I probably would have, except for the fact that Janice came in all torn up and crying about her mother needing a kidney transplant and some shit about finding out that Terri was her real sister. That on top of all the bullshit that I've been putting her through, I had no choice but to try and be here for her. I knew that Anthony would be pissed off, but I felt I could fix it later. Fortunately enough for Janice's mom her one working kidney has been holding out fine, but just to be on top of things they began to run tests on Janice and Terri's kidney's and guess what we found. The bitch Janice is pregnant, almost six weeks at that. I can't believe this. She's running around this motherfucker as happy as a sissy with a bag full of dicks, expecting me to be as happy as she is. I even looked the bitch dead in her eyes, and asked her if she had ever cheated on me. I mean after all the cheating and staying out bullshitting, that I've been doing, not to mention my falling in love with Anthony I would have had no choice but to forgive her, finally come clean and move on. Well to my surprise the bitch looked me right back in the eyes and lied. Lied like a dog, she did. No baby, she said no matter what we been through, I could never cheat on you, I love you Derrick with all my heart. Lying bitch, unless she's the Virgin Mary about to rehave the baby Jesus, somebody has put some dick in her ass, and made a baby, I know mother fucking well that's not my baby, it's just downright physically impossible. That's why I'm on my way to see Anthony now. I haven't seen him in quite some time, he barely says anything to me at work; he tries to avoid me completely and I just can't take it anymore, the phone rung about three times before he picked up. Hello, He said sounding sexy as ever. Hi baby, I said sounding exhausted. Derrick, why are you calling me when I asked you not to, he said. Come on baby, please don't do this to me I pleaded, you know that you are all that I have Anthony I said, you are the only one that really knows me and I need to talk to you right now, it can't wait open the garage please I'm outside.

CH. 18

JANICE...

It's been a strange two months for me. Fortunately enough my mom is holding her own, her one working kidney is doing better than was expected. Dialysis is not in the picture right now. Terri and I made arrangements to be tested immediately. Amazingly I was a great match, but I pray that her strong kidney holds out until after my baby is born. Yep you heard me right, finally Derrick and I are about to be parents. He's not as happy as I am about it but I'm not worried, as soon as he sets eyes on our child that will all change. He's even been coming in every night and I'm sure that he stopped seeing that gay guy Anthony too. I never mentioned to him that I saw him that night and now I'm glad that I didn't. Something strange did happen though; Derrick came to me shortly after I told him that we were about to become parents and asked me the strangest question. I don't know where it came from, but he asked me had I ever cheated on him. I'm not the cheating type and he knows that. Besides it was only that one time with Marvin, he's the guy whose brother Derrick was so called engaged to. It only happened that one time and nobody knows except the two of us. I don't see any reason to fuck up my family for one mistake. I don't feel bad for lying to Derrick either. Why should I? Shit after all did he tell me the truth about all the bitches and even possibly guys that he was out there fucking? There is something to worry about though; after confiding in my Dr. about Derrick possibly being gay he suggested that I get tested for HIV every three to four months for the next year. Now do you see why I don't feel bad about lying to him, at least my lie wasn't life threatening like his. He may not be happy about our baby, but I don't care, I am. He's here with us and that's all that matters to me right now. The phone rang and I knew before I answered it that it was my sister, that sounded so good to me, my sister, after all these years, next to finding out that I was carrying Derrick's child that was the greatest thing that ever happened to me. I answered and just as I thought it was Terri. I need to talk to you, she said. Is there something wrong Terri, I asked nervously? She sounded very upset. Derricks not home and I don't know when to expect him back you can come right over, I replied. Why don't you come over to my house, Terri answered back? I don't want to risk running into Derrick's trifling ass for one, and for two, when was the last time you seen your handsome nephew, she asked? Now you know, that I can't resist a chance to spend time with Brandon, I answered, but as far as you and Derrick goes, the two of you have got to find some common ground Terri. As much as I love you Janice, Terri replied, I could never see Derrick and I ever having any type of common ground. How can you say that Terri, I asked? You're my only sister, I'm about to have a child with this man and marry him. That's just my point, said Terri; when does his lousy ass plan on marrying you Janice? He's not even happy about this baby. Why in the hell do you think he's going to go through with this marriage? I will be there in fifteen minutes Terri, I said as I hung up the phone. My sister just doesn't like Derrick for nothing in the world. If he saved her life, I don't think she would change her mind about him. I'm not going to let her bad mouth him anymore. I don't know what it's going to take for her to understand that I love him with all my heart and I'm not about to lose him now. My stomach started feeling queasy as I pulled into Terri's driveway. The front door was already open only the screen was shut. I started to back out and call her back with an excuse why I couldn't make it. As my luck would have it, right at that very moment Terri opened the screen door and walked out onto the porch carrying two glasses of what looked like iced tea. Get your ass out of that car, she yelled, you think that I didn't know that you were about to back out of my driveway. Can you read my mind, I joked backed at her? Yes she answered, I can read your mind. I don't want to talk about Derrick Terri I said, it's no secret that you don't like him, no matter what he does or doesn't do. The truth of the matter is that we're happier than we ever were; we're having a child, getting married and he doesn't even spend the night out anymore.

What about the fact that he's gay Janice, she asked? What about that, if he's not spending the night out anymore Terri it evidently means that he's not seeing anyone else, not even that guy, I said in his defense. It doesn't take all night to do anything Janice, she yelled at me! What do you have for a brain, she screamed? I don't want to hear this right now Terri, I said as I heard my nephew began to cry from someplace inside the house, our loud voices must have woke him up. Well we are going to talk about this, right here, right now, she said opening the door and going inside. Why are you bringing this up right now today, I asked her against my better judgment? I don't know what it was but something inside of me was just screaming, run outside, jump in your car and get the hell out of here! Terri came back carrying Brandon in her arms. Before I could even ask her she handed him over to me and said, sit down Janice, I have something to tell you and it ain't pretty.

CH. 19

TERRI...

I feel like the worst person in the world, but hell what can I do? Why am I always the one that has to do the dirty work or bear the bad news? I don't care if my sister has to raise her child alone; I'd rather that, than her playing second to a man. I don't want her later on down the line dying of aids, if that's not already the case. She told me that she has to be tested for HIV for the next year, and she's carrying a baby. That's too much to go through. I found out that I was wrong about my husband Todd having an affair, after confronting him with that number I found in his pocket. At first I was reluctant to confront him about it. I sat out in my driveway for what seemed like hours, but was probably more like fifteen-twenty minutes. I went straight into his little home office with phone number in hand. What is this Todd, I asked all prepared to chew his ass up and spit him out. Where did you find that, he asked with a relieved look on his face. Why is this woman's phone number in your pocket and who is she, I asked? Suddenly a smile crept across his face. What's funny, I asked? You are he replied, if I didn't know any better Terri, I would say that you were jealous and that you think that you have caught me doing something wrong. I stood there feeling kind of confused but still waiting on an explanation. Well he said finally, sorry to disappoint you but that number belongs to a co-worker of mine, whose sixteen year old daughter is searching for babysitting jobs, call her and check it out Ms. Detective. I called immediately and he was telling the truth. The teenage girl was ecstatic that I had finally called and enquired of her services. I went through some details with her before finally getting off the phone. I think that someone owes me an apology for their thoughts, Todd said smiling at me. Whatever, I replied. I'll bet that you and Janice already had me tried and sentenced didn't you, he asked? I just laughed it off and relaxed for the first time since I had found that number in his pants pocket. That night though I had got to thinking, what if Derrick has really changed?

I had begun to feel like maybe I should back off and leave the two of them alone. I decided that I at least had to be sure that he wasn't still carrying on his relationship with Anthony, so I decided to go and ask Marvin, Anthony's brother about it. Well I didn't have to ask anyone, anything because as soon as I was in sight of Anthony's condo, what did I see but Derrick's snake ass pulling into the garage. That's why I called my sister and told her to get over to my place ASAP. It's about time for her to face this shit head on and to move on with her life. I told her what I saw earlier that day, she instantly began to cry. God knows that I didn't want to upset her like that but I had to. What do I do, she asked? Hell I didn't know the answer. I told her about the suspicions that I had about Todd and how I just confronted him head on. She said that a head on confrontation wouldn't suffice with Derrick because he would only lie, like he's been doing all along. I agreed. She stopped crying and gave me a hug. What was that for, I asked. That's for always being here for me, she said also for being the best sister in the world. I don't know about the best sister thing, I replied but I try. Janice I hope that you know that it hurts me to see you go through this especially at a time like this. I know that you take no pleasure in doing this Terri, Janice replied but if you don't make me face this thing and get it over with I will procrastinate forever, and you know that. Ok where do we start? We can go over there right now, I said. What about Brandon, she asked? I can the sitter, I told her. I would like to go and visit Marvin first, that way I can have some idea what I'm up against. You can't just pop up over there, I said. I have his phone number Terri, she said. When did this happen, I asked her. The night we met, she replied. I wish you would have gone to breakfast like you started to do in the first place, I said to her. If I had done that Terri, she said I would have never known what I was up against right? Yeah I guess you are right about that, I replied. Don't worry sis; I said somehow, someway, we will get through this.

CH. 20

MARVIN…

Janice called and asked if she could come over. Funny thing I haven't been able to stop thinking about her. She is beautiful inside and out. I don't think that I've ever thought about a woman so much in my life. I hope that she didn't get upset about what happened. I know that I shouldn't have taken advantage of her like I did. I swear I was trying my best, not to put the moves on her. We were talking about my brother Anthony and her fiancé Derrick and their twisted gay relationship. I was upset, she was upset and the next thing you know we were tongue wrestling to my bedroom, where we finished it off with the horizontal tango, three times. I wanted her to spend the night but her girlfriend called with some kind of emergency. The next thing I know she was showering, dressing and talking hurriedly. I didn't get a word in inch wise. Now she's coming over, I hope that it's not to talk about Derrick Geter and Anthony. What does a woman like her see in Derrick's feminine ass anyway, in love with a man when he has a woman like her at home? Anthony even said that she was fine. He evidently saw her leaving that day; he came running his ass over here as fast as he could trying to find out about her and her friend. That's the Anthony I know. This new gay Anthony that's anticipating marrying a man is a stranger to me. I didn't tell him who she was though because we ended up getting into this big fight. He got upset with me. I just had to come right out and tell him the truth about how I felt. I thought that maybe I had got to him, because I haven't been seeing Derrick around lately. That was a little too good to be true, because this morning guess what I saw? Yep you guessed it, Derrick pulling up into Anthony's garage. I saw him leave right before Janice called me, so I told her to call me from her cell, so that I can open my garage and she can pull in. I don't know if Derrick's coming back over to Anthony's and I don't want any drama, not when she's here anyway. I can't imagine what it's like to be her and in her situation right now. The phone is ringing, I know it's her. I answer the phone and hit the garage door opener at the same time. Much to my surprise, she looks as if she has put on a few pounds; don't get me wrong, it looked good on her. Hi Marvin, she said trying to manage a smile. You don't look to happy, I say to her hanging up her purse and jacket. Happy is a word that hasn't been in my vocabulary for quite some time now, she replied. Once again I notice that her hips has spread a bit, damn she looked sexier than before. How about a cognac, I asked trying my hardest to keep my mind off those hips. I was really feeling Janice, it's just that her beauty overpowers everything else around her. I have never reacted to a woman this way before. I really shouldn't be drinking, she replied after all that's not the reason I'm here. There had better be a good reason that you can't share a drink with me, considering your love me and leave me routine you pulled on me last time, I said. She smiled at me looking embarrassed as hell. I'm sorry; I said, I didn't mean to embarrass you. No she said looking off in the distance; I acted like a tramp, maybe that's the reason I haven't called. I picked up the phone to call a hundred times, I just couldn't make myself go through with it, she said. That's one of the reasons that I should pass on that drink. I made us both a drink anyway. I walked over to the sofa where she was sitting; put the drinks down on the end table and sat as close to her as I could without touching her. I know what we did was surprising but I don't regret it and I won't apologize for it, I said to her. She finally turned around and looked at me. Right away her light brown eyes stole the show and my feelings began to stir. I just wanted to grab her, hold her in my arms and tell her that everything was going to be all right. Earth to Marvin, she said snapping her fingers in my face. Sorry what was that, I replied finally coming out of my trance. Did you hear a word that I said, she asked? Honestly, I answered I didn't. That's what I mean, she said. What, I asked a little concerned about her tone of voice. How can you listen to me, actually take me serious, she asked?

When you met me, I jumped in your car like some common hoe, then to top off the night I find out that my fiancé is sleeping with your brother and as if that's not enough, I come over here and jump in bed with you, she said starting to cry. Angrily I slammed my glass down on the table. It must have scared her because she almost jumped out of her skin. I'm sorry, she said, as she was about to stand. I grabbed her and held her in my arms. At first she resisted, but she gave in and just cried unstoppable for quite some time. I let go of her just long enough to go and grab some Kleenex. I walked back into the room and handed them to her. Ok Miss Lady, I said you have had your say, now I think it's about time that I have mine. She looked up with her face all red and puffy from all the crying. I'm sorry, she repeated herself, but I cut her off in mid sentence. What does a brother have to do to get a word in with you, I asked jokingly? Ok, she said go ahead and talk. First of all I said, when we first met we were on our way to grab some breakfast. I personally don't see anything wrong with that. You were the one that was decent enough to acknowledge that you had a man at home. Don't get me wrong now I was about to say and do anything that I possibly could to get you to stay in my car and go eat with me. Though something in the back of my mind tells me that it wouldn't have worked, I said. Derrick showing up at that exact moment and time just tells me that God was trying to tell you something. Neither one of us had any control over that, I said. Before I met you that night this relationship with Derrick and Anthony was tearing me apart inside, but after that night, though it still bothered me for some reason you began to preoccupy my thoughts. I know that it's a little far fetched for you to believe, because I found it hard to believe myself. The day I saw you and your friend out there playing detective I had to do a double take to make sure that I wasn't seeing things, I said. Now it didn't take a rocket scientist to know why the two of you were there. All I know is that I had to take advantage of the moment, I said to her. As for what happened between the two of us, hell I was hurting, you were hurting. They both hurt us, so we turned to each other for a moment to ease our pain. I will not let you sit here and make something ugly out of it, I told her. I know that you don't just go around having one night stands I said, that's what I do. I run around and try to conquer every piece of loose pussy that I can, and I do a lot of other things that I'm not so proud of when it comes to women, I said. Things like what, she asked. As fate would have it before I got to answer that question my doorbell rang. What came next not only shocked the fuck out of me, but it brought a whole new meaning to the past coming back to haunt you.

CH. 21

ANTHONY...

Derrick and I had a long talk earlier. Well he tried to talk to me but I couldn't really hear him. I mean I love Derrick and all but there's just too much drama attached to him. He did admit to me that, the woman he was living with is his girlfriend and not his roommate. He kept going on about her cheating on him or something. I really wasn't listening. I can't concentrate on shit, but how Marvin talked to me the last time I saw him. I went over there with good intention in my heart, to ease his mind about my situation. Did he hear me though? Hell no. he wanted to get all self righteous about how he couldn't talk about it right now and how I had hurt him so much. As far as Derrick and his cheating bitch, who in the fuck does he think he is to judge that woman anyway? When or if she ever finds out the truth about him, she will probably need therapy for the rest of her life. I was going to go over there and tell her the truth about his lying ass, but then he told me that her mother was going through a serious medical condition. I couldn't imagine going through something like that with my mom. As bad as I wanted someone to hurt right along with me when Derrick said that he was staying there to be by her side, I knew that it wasn't her that was making me ache inside. No it wasn't her. It was that lying, manipulative ass Derrick. Loving him as much as I do, doesn't help the situation any either, neither does having to see him at work everyday. Now all of a sudden he thinks that I'm going to welcome him back with open arms? Hell no. this time I'm going to just let it burn, at least that's just what I'm going to keep telling myself. Back to Marvin my brother, my twin brother, that's now so concerned with what I do in my personal life. Well now that I think back he always was, wasn't he? He had the nerve to refer to me as sick. Isn't that something! If anyone around here is sick, it's his sick, distorted, twisted, perverted ass. I think after all these years he's finally ran into a real woman. One with some class, nothing like the tramps he's accustomed to. She's a real looker to, at least from the quick glance that I got of her leaving his condo and jumping into a waiting car with her girlfriend. I went over shortly after seeing her leave for some brother talk. It's nothing unusual. After all we are twins, we share everything. Much to my surprise he didn't even want to discuss Miss Goody two shoes, let alone how good the action was. I think the day has finally come, after all these years for my brother to know, how it feels to have your heart completely ripped out of your chest; grin, bear it, and keep living life like nothing ever happened. For me it couldn't have come at a better time. I saw Miss Goody two shoes going into Marvin's place earlier. He's trying to be real discreet, having her pull into the garage and all. The fact that he even invited a woman into his precious home more than once was shocking. He's the king of one night stands. Yeah he must really be feeling this one. I down a couple more shots of cognac to build up my nerves. Then I grab my house keys and put them in my pocket as I head over to Marvin's to join the party, lights, camera, and motherfucking action.

CH. 22

TERRI...

I can't believe what Janice is sitting here telling me. Evidently this Anthony motherfucker is a damn lunatic or something. From what I can get out of her between her sobbing and crying, both he and his brother is a couple of sick bastards. I was pacing the floor, wondering what was going on with her over at that Marvin guy's house, when all of a sudden she pulls up in the driveway, blowing the horn like Satan himself was chasing her. I hurried out of the door because I didn't know what was going on, Derrick could have been chasing her or something; after all she never did call me like she said that she would. Anyway like I said I had been pacing the floor going back and forward looking out of the window when finally, I saw her car come racing up the street. Once I got her inside and calmed her down, she asked me if I could get her some water. After what seemed like an eternity, she wiped her face and began to talk. What happened, I asked? I don't even know where to start, she replied. Did you see Derrick, I asked? No, she answered. Then she started telling me how she had gone over to Marvin's and how they were having a heart to heart discussion. I didn't understand because to my knowledge they had only seen each other once or twice. Well they say that you never really know anyone no matter how long you've known them and today, I found this to be true. Well, well, well, come to find out that little Ms. Dingbat Janice wasn't that much of a dingbat after all. I left her over there to have a conversation with old fine ass and they did a lot more than talk. I must admit that I was happy about it. So what in the hell happened tonight, I asked once again hoping that Janice wasn't silly enough to pop up at this mans home without calling. I didn't know if he had a woman or something like that. Come to find out it was worse than I thought. Janice told me that she felt uncomfortable about them sleeping together that one night. She said that Marvin confessed to having genuine feelings for her and she was shocked by this. I was getting very impatient with all of her procrastinating. I told her to get to the point and she started to cry again. Everything was going great she said, until Marvin made a comment about how he never had real feelings for a woman before. He said that he had done some twisted things to them, so I asked him what he meant by that. Did he do something to hurt you, I asked now nervous as hell? I would have never imagined what she told me next. According to Janice before Marvin could answer her question, there was a loud knock at his door. Don't tell me it was his girlfriend, I said excitedly. Well I was wrong it wasn't a woman it was his brother Anthony. At first I thought that he had found out who Janice was and confronted, threatened her or something like that. But that wasn't the case; she said that he had no idea who she was. Now I was on the edge of my sofa. She said that she was nervous about being in the same room with Derrick's lover, especially when he asked Marvin to introduce him to his friend. Marvin tried to get rid of him by hurriedly introducing her as a close friend named Jade. She said that Anthony came over and shook her hand like a perfect gentleman and that he was much more handsome in person. Then she said that Marvin asked Anthony if he could come back at another time? That's when according to Janice things got a little weird. What's wrong big brother Anthony asked Marvin, Ms. Jade don't know how we get down? I was so scared Janice said trembling, I had no idea what in the hell he was talking about, so I asked Marvin what was going on. Marvin said that everything was fine and that his brother evidently had been drinking or something. Well yes Anthony said, I have been drinking a bit, but I can still get down it's never stopped me before. Janice said that she once again asked Marvin; what was going on. My brother was just leaving, Marvin told her. He walked across the room and opened the door, cueing Anthony that his time was up. I thought that they were about to get into some big fight or something, said Janice. But Anthony walked out without hesitation. Marvin apologized for his brother's actions but I was still nervous, she said. Marvin what just happened here, Janice said that she asked him? She said he told her that he would explain it to her later.

She told me that Marvin grabbed her and held her in his arms after noticing how shaken up she was. It felt so good that I instantly forgot everything, she said. It's been so long since a man has held me like that. Derrick doesn't even sleep in our bed, since I told him about the baby, she said starting to cry again. They ended up in bed again. Janice doesn't even get down like this, I thought to myself. Anyway she went on to say that she thought she heard a strange sound in the living room, but passed it off as her imagination knowing that they were the only ones there. She said that once they were finished making love, Marvin decided to get some carry out from the Chinese restaurant around the corner. Once he was gone she drifted back off to sleep. She said that she wasn't sure how long she'd been sleeping, but that she knew it wasn't long enough for Marvin to be back already. She was still pretty drowsy; therefore she said that she didn't give it much thought. Well she should have because he pulled off his clothes and slid in bed beside her, and blindfolded her, she said. Blindfolded you, I asked not understanding at all. Yes Terri she said blindfolded me and started kissing me like I've never been kissed before. So old Marvin's a freak, what's wrong with that Janice I asked? Shit he need to come over here and talk to Todd, we could use some extra excitement in the bedroom, I said. Even though I was a little uncomfortable with it, I must admit it did feel good, she continued. She went on to say that he was just about to penetrate her, when she heard Marvin's voice yell, "What in the fuck are you doing Anthony?" she said that she pulled that blindfold off as fast as she could and there behind her lay Anthony with his dick sticking straight up in the air and Marvin standing in the doorway. Anthony jumped up and grabbed a nearby towel and wrapped it around his bottom half. What happened next, I asked barely able to believe what I was hearing? Marvin rushed at Anthony and they began to struggle around on the floor while I was putting my clothes on as fast as I could, she said. Once Janice got dressed she tried to pull Marvin and Anthony apart. She said that she begin screaming to them to please break it up. Then she said that they both stopped struggling and came to a stand, Marvin looking all disheveled and Anthony's nose was bleeding. I just ran up out of there as fast as I could embarrassed as hell; she said. That's why I drove over here so fast. I will never speak to Marvin again, Janice added and Derrick can have that fucking pervert also.

CH. 23

JANICE...

How in the hell did I get in the middle of this bullshit? Anytime something appears too good to be true it always is. Now I understand what Marvin meant when he said that he does twisted things with women. I told Terri part of the story. Well actually I told her the truth. I just didn't leave when I said that I did. I had begun to walk out of the door when Marvin ran up and grabbed me. I started to scream for him to let go of me. Please baby listen to me, he begged. I don't think that I want to hear this Marvin, I replied. Why not, Anthony asked, going to the bathroom to get some tissue for his bloody nose. How did you get in here, Marvin asked his brother? How long have we had keys to each others place, Anthony asked right back? That really isn't the issue; Marvin replied. What in the hell is wrong with you Anthony? What is wrong with me, Anthony yelled back? I'm sick and tired of you talking down to me. Who in the fuck do you think you are Marvin, he yelled? I don't think that this is the right time to discuss this Anthony, he said. As a matter of fact Marvin added, I don't even want to talk to you at all right now. I think that this is the perfect time to talk about it Marvin, Anthony replied. Since when do you punch me in the face for pulling the switch on some broad, he asked? She's not that type of woman, Marvin answered him angrily. Anyway you're engaged to be married, isn't that enough for you, Marvin asked? Not to mention that you're dating a... but before Marvin could finish, Anthony cut him off in mid sentence and said; we're not here to talk about my personal life Marvin. Since when is any woman not the type? Is she suppose to be special or something, he asked? Yes, Marvin answered as a matter of fact she is Anthony, I care for her a great deal. That's bullshit Marvin and you know it, yelled Anthony. I don't care what you think anymore Anthony, Marvin replied calming down a great deal but looking at Anthony as if he could literally wring his neck. Is that what you meant when you said that you have done twisted things with women, I asked him? Is this what you and your brother do, get unsuspecting women in your beds then switch up on them during sex? We used to do things like that; Marvin answered me looking as though he was sinking on dry land. We have never done it without each other's consent and baby I would never play you like that, he said to me. I swear to you, that I really care about you more than you know, he said. Why Anthony, Marvin asked turning to his brother with tears in his eyes. Why would you do something like this to me? Come in my home and try and violate my guest in such a manner? That's the shit that I'm talking about; Anthony said starting to tear up also. Why in the hell do you keep acting all judgmental with me Marvin he yelled, just because you really care about a woman means she's off limits? Is that what you're trying to say Marvin, Anthony begin to yell? If you have to ask me some shit like that Anthony you are more fucked up than I thought you were, Marvin replied. Do you think that if your situation was different than it is that I would come across the street, get in your bed and fuck you're fiancé Anthony, Marvin asked? You already did Anthony answered, with a sad look on his face. What the fuck do you mean I already did, Marvin yelled I'm not fucking gay, I've never touched that... once again Anthony cut him off in mid sentence. Don't act like you don't remember her, he screamed! I loved her more than life itself and she loved me the same. But you just couldn't take that could you Marvin; Anthony continued you just had to fuck her. All of a sudden Marvin got a look on his face as if he had seen a ghost. You knew, he asked Anthony in a voice barely above a whisper? Yes, Anthony answered I knew. Marvin was referring to Karen Anthony's high school sweetheart; he had witnessed her and his brother Anthony making passionate love early one morning, while his parents were away on vacation. After opening the door and standing there watching the show for longer than he should have, he decided that he must have her, and he did. When did you find out, Marvin asked looking sadly into his brother's eyes? I figured it out a couple of days later when she asked me to blindfold her again and fuck her from the back, like I did that day in my parents' bathroom. Is that why the two of you broke up, Marvin asked but I think that he had already figured out the answer to that question? What do you think; Anthony asked, looking tired, weary and defeated. I couldn't marry her after my brother had fucked her so good that she wanted me to repeat the performance, he said. Furthermore once she figured out what happened she was embarrassed and angry with herself for not knowing the difference, as if somehow she could have known. She transferred schools and moved away. I never seen or heard from her ever again, said Anthony heading for the door. I know that it doesn't mean much to you right now said Marvin, but I am sorry for that day; and more so now than you will ever know. I started to cry because I began to wonder, what if Marvin hadn't done that to his brother so many years ago, would he and I be going through the shit we are going through right now. I wondered if Anthony thought that fucking a man was the only way out of sharing his lovers with his brother. I believe that the same thought was going through Marvin's mind. I picked up my purse and headed out of the door. Marvin looked as if he wanted to stop me, but he didn't. I'm sorry that I did that to you Ms. Jade; Anthony said looking at me with the saddest eyes I've ever seen. So am I, I said walking out of the door. The garage door went up so I assumed that Marvin had gotten up and pushed the opener. It's just that once I got in the car I broke down in tears and headed straight for Terri. I feel like I'm falling in love with the very person that's ruining my life. How do I get myself in situations like this? I had a feeling that Derrick wouldn't be home when I got there. I was sure that just like I ran to Terri, that Anthony would surely run to Derrick and I was right, he wasn't here.

CH. 24

DERRICK...

I called Anthony and poured my heart out to him earlier this evening. I couldn't help it I was so mad at the way Janice is running around here all smiles telling everyone that I fathered her baby. She's a lying ass bitch, is what she is. I'm not tolerating this shit any longer. It kills me to think that I was willing to give up Anthony for her. I was beginning to think that I had messed up with him altogether, because even though he let me come over to his place, he was still cold and distant. I can't say that I blame him though, besides at work, where he goes out of his way to avoid me, we haven't spoke in a while. As I was saying, he let me come over and heard me out for the most part but I think that he was relieved, when I left. He has a twin brother that lives across the street from him. I've never met him or anything like that. He did approach us one day expecting to be introduced, I guessed. But Anthony just hurried him off. Our situation isn't the most comfortable one at all. Anyway I came home and the bitch wasn't here. I wonder where she is. Probably out with whoever put that baby up in her ass. I know that I'm wrong for feeling this way about Janice, after all the stuff that I have put her through. Honestly I feel hurt and jealous. I just can't believe that she's lying to me like this, that's all. Like I said I was beginning to think that Anthony wanted nothing to do with me anymore. I was sitting at home wondering what he was doing at that moment and guess what? Evidently he was thinking of me too, because all of a sudden my cell phone rang and it was Anthony. You should have seen the look on my face when I saw his number on my caller I D. I was ecstatic to hear his voice. He asked me if I could come over. He said that it had been a hectic day for him and that he just wanted to be close to me. Well of course I grabbed my keys and ran out as fast as I could. All the way here I was smiling and thinking about, how lucky I was to have someone like him in my life. He must have been watching for me in the window because as soon as I turned the corner, his garage door went up.

Anthony greeted me at the door with a kiss, and went to get me a cup of coffee. I asked him what was wrong and he burst into tears. He grabbed me, pulled me down on the sofa and we made love for the first time in months. It felt like heaven. Once we came up for air, Anthony began to tell me about his brother Marvin. He told me about his first love and how close they were. He told me that he was about to get engaged to her in his junior year and marry her right after graduation. He also said that until I came along he had never had feelings like this for another human being. I sat there and begin to wonder how in the hell did I get myself in this sick twisted ass relationship with Janice, and more so than that how in the hell do I get myself out of it. Are you listening to anything that I'm saying Derrick? Anthony's voice sounded like it was coming from miles away. Yes, I answered coming out of my daydream and turning to look at him. I hadn't heard a word that he'd said. I wasn't listening baby I apologize, I said to him. I was telling you how my brother Marvin faked an asthma attack and had me run out to the pharmacy; because he was suppose to be out of inhalers. Why, I asked confused? Why you think, Anthony replied, so that he could catch my fiancé coming out of the shower. Don't tell me that he pretended be you, I said feeling that I already knew the answer to that question. That's exactly what he did, pretended to be me, blindfolded her, walked her back in the bathroom and fucked her, he said. How did you find out, I asked? One night we were about to make love at her parents house, she asked me if next time I can bring my blindfolds, and repeat our performance over the basin, in the bathroom, like I did at my parents house a few days earlier. I felt like shit when I figured out what must have went down. I might have even tried to get over it and still marry her after I dealt with my brother. The thing that hurt me the most and made me just tell her what had happened, leave her alone and wait for the right moment to get him back was that Karen kept going on and on about how good it was and how it was the best love that we had ever made. Are you kidding me, I asked in total shock? No, you heard me right, he answered that's exactly what he did. I didn't know what to say to him to make him feel any better, so I just sat there not knowing what to say or do. I can't believe that you never confronted him, I said. He told me that he never told Marvin, he and Karen just broke it off, shortly after she transferred to another county and they never saw or spoke to one another ever again. I asked him if he missed her. He said that he used to miss her so much that he wanted to die but finally he got passed it. I love my brother Anthony went on to say, but I swear on everything inside of me, I had to pay him back. Don't tell me that you slept with his woman for revenge, I said. That was the plan, Anthony said. The fucked up thing about that is he never gave a fuck about the women he slept with. Anthony said that Marvin was always all too happy to share his female companions, until lately. I asked him what in the hell had happened lately? He told me that Marvin had been seeing some woman named Jade that he was being very secretive about. Anthony said that she was very attractive and classy. Evidently Anthony had gone over there to get invited to the party. Much to his surprise Marvin wasn't sharing anymore, as a matter of fact he just introduced her and hurried Anthony's ass out of there. He said that he left but crept back in with the key that his brother had given him some time ago. Once Marvin and his lady were done doing the do, she sent him out for Chinese food. According to Anthony that's when he made his move. It hurt me to hear him say that he went into the room, slid in bed with her, blindfolded her, and began having foreplay. I just sat there trying to pretend that what was being said wasn't tearing my heart out. I was glad when he got to the part where Marvin came in and caught him. They all argued for hours. Anthony said that Marvin was so angry with him that he told him in tears how scantless, lowdown and no good that he was for what he had done. Anthony said that he begin to cry also and told Marvin that he knew everything that happened with Karen all those years ago and that he's always known. He said that Marvin was very shocked and sad to hear what he was saying to him but that he also began to cry with him. This shit is deep I thought to myself while reaching over, kissing him and we starting back making love all over again.

CH. 25

MARVIN...

I know that I got what I deserved today. I just wish that Janice hadn't got caught up in it. I know that there's no way in the hell that she would want to hear anything that I had to say to her right now. I brought this on myself all those years ago, when I screwed Anthony's girl. I had no idea all this time that he knew. Why had he held it in all this time? Why hadn't he come to me? We could have dealt with this then and I wouldn't be sitting here with my heart hurting. I could only imagine what Janice must have felt. The same guy that's sleeping with her man was a split second away from screwing her also. As if this day hasn't been dramatic enough, I look outside and see Derrick's car pulling into Anthony's garage. Why doesn't Derrick just leave Janice alone? I wish that he would just move in with Anthony and leave her alone. I wonder what Anthony would have said if he had known who Janice really was? I feel that I have nothing to lose and they both need to know what they are doing to her. I grabbed my keys and headed across the street. He started this and tonight I was going to end it. I know that what I did was wrong, but he could have come to me like a man. Instead he chose to terrify the only woman that I ever cared for. I love her and it's about time that I start acting like it. I didn't know what was going to happen, as I knocked on Anthony's door for the third time. I knew that they were in there. Finally Anthony yelled, who is it? He opened the door once he realized that it was me. This is not a good time Marvin, he said trying to close the door on me. I stuck my foot in the door to keep it from closing. This is the best time, I said. He stepped aside and let me in. I have company, Derrick's here he informed me. I know I saw him when he pulled into the garage I told him. Is this suppose to be some kind of retaliation for what happened earlier, he asked? That would be childish, I answered. That's exactly what I was thinking, he said. Actually I wanted to tell you the truth about my company, I told him. I apologize again for what I did earlier Marvin, he said. But like I said, I have company and this is not the time. This involves Derrick also; therefore it's the perfect time and he needs to come out here and listen to what I have to say, I repeated. I already told Derrick what happened today, Anthony said. I told him what you done to me all those years ago and about my effortless attempt at revenge, sneaking into your place trying to fuck your friend. How did he take that, I asked? He took it pretty well I guess, what does it matter to you we have our own problems Marvin, said Anthony trying to get me out of the door. I would like to speak with him, I said once again. Fine said Anthony giving in, like I knew that he eventually would. I told you that I was older than him by only eight minutes but I could always get him to see things my way whether he wanted to or not. He went into his bedroom, closing the door behind him. My stomach started to turn just at the thought of my brother having a man in his bed. Finally he returned and said that Derrick would be right out he just needed a moment to get himself together. I began to wonder how much time a man needs to pull on some pants. Then I remembered that he was a homosexual, so I don't know what rules they live by. What is it that's so important that you need to talk to Derrick about, Anthony asked after all you don't even know him. You're right, I answered I don't know him, but I know someone that does and she deserves better than this. Are you talking about that Janice woman that you met at the club that night, Anthony asked? Yes, I answered. I didn't know that you were still keeping in touch with her, he said. What have you told her, he asked? Please let Derrick handle this himself, he said. I can't do that; I replied, I'm in too deep at this point. What do you mean you're in too deep, Anthony asked. What I mean I said just as Derrick walked out of the bedroom, is that the woman you climbed in bed with today was not my woman; it was Janice, Derrick's woman. What the fuck did you say, Derrick yelled while charging at me with all of his strength Anthony got in the middle because believe me I wanted a piece of his lying, cheating faggot ass, as bad as he wanted a piece of mine. After what seemed like forever Anthony managed to calm things down.

How did you meet Janice, Derrick asked taking a big gulp of the cognac that Anthony had fixed the three of us. I met her at that new club downtown, I told him. We had a couple of drinks and I convinced her to go to breakfast with me, I continued. Are you trying to tell me that Janice actually got in your car, Derrick asked in total surprise? Yes she got in I answered, but we never made it to breakfast. What happened, he asked? You happened, I answered him. What the hell do you mean I happened, Derrick asked looking frightened as hell? She started talking about having a man at home that she loved and how he didn't deserve to be cheated on. She was about to make a quick exit at the exact time you decided to pull up, I continued. By this time Derrick was sweating like hell, once again he took a big gulp of his drink and passed his glass to Anthony for a refill. Let me get this straight he said looking at me as if he couldn't believe what he was hearing. Janice was about to leave a club, late at night, with a man that she had just met. Is that what you are telling me, he asked? That's exactly what I'm saying, I replied. You just happened to pull up at that moment and she started ducking down in my seat. I asked her why she was ducking and she told me that you were her boyfriend. Derrick turned to see how Anthony was going to react to what he had heard. Is that how you found out that I was lying about Janice being my roommate, Derrick asked Anthony? Yes, Anthony answered him. Why didn't you come to me then, Derrick asked him? I was waiting on you to come clean with me, Anthony answered. I don't know what to say, Derrick replied. What happened after she told you that I was her boyfriend, Derrick asked looking as though he had somehow already figured out the answer. I told her that she could have come up with a better excuse than that because you were my brother's fiancé. Derrick looked as though the life had been knocked out of him as he slowly polished off his drink, stood up and headed back into Anthony's bedroom.

CH. 26

JANICE...

Just like I figured, Derrick wasn't home when I got here. There's no doubt in my mind where he is. I don't know what to think or do right now. I felt so violated by that bastard Anthony. I keep asking myself what if Marvin wouldn't have walked in when he did. I was in total shock when he was standing in the bedroom doorway asking Anthony what in the hell was going on? My blood froze. I swear I could not tell the difference. Believe it or not I kind of feel sorry for Anthony. I also understand what that girl Karen must have felt, very embarrassed and violated. Why did Marvin do something that horrible to his brother? Why did it have to come back on me? I know that I shouldn't have been making love to Marvin anyway, me being pregnant and all. I just couldn't resist it. That is one irresistible man. The chemistry between us is absolutely phenomenal I think that I'm falling, oh hell, who am I fooling? I'm so in love with Marvin that I don't even give a fuck that Derrick probably is over there with Anthony right at this very moment. I don't care anymore at this point. I wish that he would just tell me the truth and move on. I went to my bathroom undressed, and took the longest, hottest shower that I've taken in a long time. I got out and as I walked into the hallway, I heard the door slam. I can't believe that Derrick was home this early. I wasn't expecting him till morning. I wonder where he went if he didn't go to Anthony's. I really don't care though. I just want to lie down, relax and think about all the good love that Marvin and I made. My thoughts were interrupted by Derrick busting up in the bedroom door. I turned around startled at how hard he hit the door. Why did you hit the door that hard, I asked him? Where have you been Janice, he asked angrily? I was over Terri's, I answered. When did you start questioning me about my whereabouts I asked? Since you started lying to me, he answered. I didn't know what to think, my mind was going off in a hundred different directions. What if Marvin told Anthony who I was? Oh my God! Instead of getting dressed

I pulled my robe back on and tied the belt around my stomach. God do I need Terri right now. I have no idea what you're talking about Derrick, I said, nervous as hell. I didn't know what to say or do. I have never been in a position like this before. I've never lied, cheated or played love games. I've always been the good girl. I must have been shaking like a crap game because Derrick walked right up to my face and asked me what I was shaking for? I'm shaking because you're up in my face, accusing me of God knows what, I replied. When did you become such a lying, cheating slut, Derrick asked? My heart skipped a beat, and my face felt hot. I was nervous and scared, I must admit but I was mad as hell. How dare this cheating ass homosexual call me out of my name? Who are you calling a lying, cheating, slut Derrick; I asked walking right up to him. I was scared but I was determined to hold my ground, after all I have been through. I thought about the fact that, throughout our entire relationship, he's been lying, cheating and staying out, not only all hours of the night, but sometimes all fucking night. I'm calling you one Janice, he replied turning red. Does your know it all Derrick bashing ass sister know how busy her little Janice angel has been lately? Unless you're going to be a man and tell me what in the hell you are talking about, I said refusing to back down, get the fuck out of my face and shut the fuck up talking to me. Who in the hell are you talking to; Derrick asked grabbing me by the arm and slamming me onto the bed. My heart jumped as I realized that he had actually put his hands on me. I knew that somehow, someway, he had found out about Marvin and me. I didn't know exactly how. I just knew that he did. I sat upright on the bed and begin to cry. I know that your skank ass ain't crying, he said in the nastiest tone you ever want to hear. I was too afraid to comment. The only thing that was going through my mind was; where was my sister because I needed her now more than ever; answer me, Derrick yelled as I sat there crying my eyes out. I don't know what to tell you, I replied between sobs. Oh now you don't know what to tell me, he said sarcastically. I looked at him with tear stained eyes. The more I looked at him, the more I couldn't stand his gay ass anymore, and since we were already in the middle of this shit, I felt that it was time to put all the cards on the table. I stood up, walked around him and headed for the kitchen. Where are you going Janice, Derrick asked? I can't believe that you put your hands on me Derrick, I said turning to face him. I'm going to dry my face, get a glass of water and call my sister. What are you calling Terri for, he asked? I'm calling her I replied to come and get me because you are right, it is time that we get everything out in the open, and after that one of us must leave, since this is my house I think we both know who that someone will be. I went to the kitchen, got a glass out of the cupboard went to the faucet and filled it up. I went to the linen closet, got a towel out and dried my face. I looked in the mirror; my eyes were once again all red and puffy. I ran my hand across my stomach and began to cry at the thought of my innocent baby being harmed. Derrick had slammed me on the bed so hard, without even giving a second thought to the well being of our child, that I had growing inside of me. I went into the living room and called Terri, she picked up on the second ring. I instantly begin to sob out of control, as I tried to tell her the events that had just taken place. I'll be there in five minutes, she said.

CH. 27

TERRI...

My heart is beating out of control. Todd is working late and it's too late to call my sitter, so I called my mom. I told her that I had an emergency and that she would have to watch Brandon for me. Of course she welcomed the opportunity and was in the window looking out as I pulled up. I knew that she would want to know what kind of emergency would have me out in the middle of the night with Brandon. I didn't have time to get into a long drawn out explanation. I just told her that it was urgent and that I would explain it to her as soon as I could. Much to my surprise she left it at that. I don't know what kind of mess Janice has gotten herself into, but it sounded serious. I could tell that she was either crying or had been crying. I also put my pistol in the glove compartment. After what she had told me earlier about Marvin and his sadistic brother, I don't know what I'm walking into. It seemed as if everything was slowing me down tonight the stop signs, the red lights and even other cars. I just couldn't seem to get there fast enough. My mind just kept running all over the place. I'm willing to bet that whatever this is about, Derrick's gay ass is smack dead in the middle of it. Much to my surprise as I pulled up into Janice's driveway, I saw a black Mercedes pull in right in front of me. I was even more stunned to see not only Marvin but what had to be his twin brother Anthony also. Before they could even park their car, I jumped out of mine with my heart beating so fast that I felt as if I would pass out at any moment. What are you two doing here, I asked? They both looked at me as if to say who in the hell are you? At that moment, I realized that I hadn't formally met either one of them. The one that must have been Marvin finally got a look on his face as if he recognized me. What in the hell is going on here, I asked? What makes you think that something's going on, Marvin asked? For one you and your brother is in my sister's driveway, I answered. Did she call you too, I asked? Is there something wrong with Janice, Marvin asked looking very concerned. I don't know, I answered him, but she called me about fifteen minutes ago very upset and now I get here and you two are here. We came to clear some things up with your sister and her fiancé, Anthony said opening his mouth for the first time since our little encounter. How dare you have the nerve to come here, I said to him. First of all you don't know me or anything about me, Anthony replied back with instant attitude. I know that your gay ass is fucking my sister's trifling fiancé, I said back to him with just as much attitude, and then you had the nerve to try to rape her, I added. Wait a minute bitch, Anthony snapped, before he could finish and I could get my pistol out of my purse, Marvin got in between us and yelled for us to shut the fuck up. Come on you two he pleaded, this is not the time to do this. This is not the time to do what, I asked? This is not the time or place to be airing out our dirty laundry, he said. You're right I said, let's take this inside. I walked up the stairs and knocked on the door, this was going to be a night to remember I thought to myself, I couldn't have imagined how much of a night to remember it was going to be.

CH. 28

ANTHONY...

I was stunned to find out that the woman in my brother's apartment was Derrick's girlfriend Janice. She was one good looking broad if I must say so myself. Marvin really has genuine feelings for her. He came over and interrupted Derrick and I from some of the best lovemaking that we've had in a while. I tried my damnest to hurry his ass up out of there, but to no avail. He was very pissed off at me about what had happened earlier. He insisted that he have a word with Derrick. I couldn't for the life of me figure out what Marvin had to say to Derrick that would be so urgent. When Derrick finally came out, Marvin stunned us both by telling us that his girlfriend was really Janice, Derrick's live-in. Derrick and I both had been absolutely clueless. I felt like a double idiot because not only had I been sleeping with this woman's partner, but while trying to get revenge on my brother for something that happened years ago, I almost slept with her also. I couldn't really say why Derrick looked so stunned. Maybe it was the way that Marvin said that he and Janice met. Funny thing about people even though they are cheating on their partners, the thought of their partners cheating on them actually takes them by surprise. That's fucked up; they want to cheat on someone but don't want to be cheated on. I didn't even get to ask him what he felt because much to my surprise he took his ass in the room, got dressed and ran up out of my house as if his ass cheeks were on fire or something. Once he left my brother and I begin to talk because there were some things that I needed to clear up with him. I told Marvin that I was not gay. Before I could get a word in he interrupted me. I started to laugh so hard that tears were coming out of my eyes. Marvin asked me how could I possibly laugh and find humor in a situation like this. You just don't know how much this is breaking my heart Anthony, he said to me. I'm even more concerned for mom and dad. What do you think that knowing that their son is about to marry another man is going to do to them, he asked? It's not going to do anything to them, I answered if you would just shut your big ass mouth for one minute, I will tell you why. Once again he interrupted. I know that you don't think that you are gay Anthony, he said. I've read about guys like you. Once again I couldn't stop myself from laughing, shut the fuck up and listen Marvin, I yelled finally catching my breath. I'm not gay. I'm not fucking a man, because Derrick is not a man, she is a woman! Marvin didn't hear me at first, because he went on to interrupt me again, but then all of a sudden he stopped talking, looked at me like I was crazy, and then sat down on the chair in the living room where we had been standing all along. I took this time to go over to the bar and pour him a triple shot of cognac. I chose a triple because what I had to tell him would require not only one triple maybe two or even three. I told him about how I had met Derrick when he came to work for our company. Derrick was a very quiet and to himself type of guy. I introduced myself and we kind of hit it off as buddies. After a while we became closer and for a while I started to think that I had gay tendencies because I found myself having feelings for him, like I would have for a woman. It scared the shit out of me so I started to stay my distance. One day we found ourselves working on the same project, and he asked me why I had been treating him like he had the plague or something. Of course I wasn't going to tell a man that I was having feelings for him. Much to my surprise he came right out and asked did I find myself attracted to him? Even though I did, I was still tempted to knock his ass out. I asked him was he some kind of fairy or something? He told me that he wasn't but I didn't believe him. I told him that I was going to get reassigned to another project because it wasn't a good idea for us to be working so close together. I didn't know exactly what it was but something was definitely out of whack. Then Derrick asked me was there someplace we could go and have a heart to heart. I said yes against my better judgment. We ended up going to a little bar down the street from our job. That's when he told me about how he had been born a woman named Carmen. Come again, said Marvin choking on his drink? I said that Derrick was originally born a woman named Carmen Geter. Carmen or Derrick as everyone knows her now grew up in foster homes here and there. She was never adopted just shuffled from family to family. The last home that she stayed in when she was sixteen consisted of a mother, father and two twelve year old twin boys. She said that she was very happy there and felt that at last she had found a family. I guess that's every foster Childs dream to be part of a real family. Well that dream ended for her real fast when the father came to her room one night and raped her. Oh my God said Marvin that must have been devastating to her. I couldn't even imagine Anthony went on. After that he started visiting her room almost every night. Where was his wife, Marvin asked? According to Carmen she worked midnights, Anthony replied. Did Derrick, I mean Carmen ever tell the wife, police or someone from the agency what was going on, Marvin asked? No, Anthony continued she ran away. Carmen said that she took some money that she had made babysitting and some money that the wife kept in the kitchen drawer for emergencies and took off. Where did she go from there, Marvin asked? He, well at that time she lived on the streets for a while until she met this guy and fell in live with him, I continued. They ended up getting married. He was a college professor and Carmen attended classes there. That's where she earned her masters in engineering. Carmen ended up getting pregnant and was about five months into the pregnancy when she found out that the professor had been having an affair with one of his female students. She was so devastated that she went into a state of depression. She ended up losing her baby in the eighth month of her pregnancy, after that she became even more depressed. The professor ended up divorcing her and sticking her into a mental institution. She then decided that she hated men and never wanted anything to do with them anymore. After being released, she legally changed her name to Derrick, started wearing her hair in braids and dressing as a man. She then went back to the university and began dating the professor's new wife for revenge. What a way to get back at a brother, said Marvin sitting on the edge of his seat amazed by the entire conversation. I know I replied, now that's some real revenge for your ass. Anyway I continued, when the professor found out that his wife was having an affair he was heartbroken and ended up going into a state of depression. That's when Derrick revealed his true identity to him. What did the professor do when he found out that the man that his new wife was having an affair with was really his ex-wife, Marvin asked? According to Derrick he was real fucked up about it, I said. The real fucked up part was when the lady found out that she had been sleeping with the woman whose husband she had stolen she had a nervous breakdown. I replied. After that he moved here, where he started working as an engineer and eventually met and fell in love with Janice, and the rest is history so far, I said. All of a sudden Marvin got a strange look on his face. Does Janice know that Derrick is a woman, he asked? She has no idea, I replied no idea whatsoever. Oh my God, Marvin said shocked, poor Janice has no idea that she's been sleeping with a woman all this time. What in the hell did she do to deserve this, Marvin asked? What makes her think that she can ruin innocent people's lives like this? She never intended to hurt Janice, I replied, she really thought she loved her things just went on and on I guess, the timing just was never right for honesty. Marvin looked at me as if I was some kind of monster or something. How in the world can you sit here and defend her, Marvin asked me? I'm not trying to defend her; I replied I'm just trying to see things from her point of view; after all I love her Marvin with all my heart I swear I do. That's another thing that confuses me, Marvin said looking at me with confusion on his face. If you are so in love with Derrick, Carmen or whoever in the hell he or she is. Why are you cheating with that other chick that leaves here almost every other morning, I asked? All of a sudden, I guess it came to him because he seemed to have lost all of his energy, as he slowly walked over to the sofa and sit down. By the look on your face, I guess you've already figured that out, I said. I'll be damned, Marvin said looking at me it's him isn't it, he asked? Yes, I answered the woman that you see me leave with in the morning is Carmen. That's why it took Derrick so long to come out of the room earlier when you wanted to speak with him, because he had to put back on his disguise I said, when we're here together there's no need for all that shit. No wonder you kept telling me to come back later, Marvin said. Well that and the fact that you interrupted some of the best love making that we've had so far, I said beginning to relax. I felt like a ton had been lifted off my shoulders. Then all of a sudden Marvin jumped up and grabbed his jacket. I've got to tell her, he said. Are you talking about Janice, I asked? Yes, he answered me with a sad look in his eyes. When are you going to tell her, I asked? Now, Marvin answered right damn now. Do you think that it's a good idea, I asked? There's no other way, Marvin answered I love her and she has a right to know. If you're going over there, I said then I'm going with you. I grabbed my jacket and my keys and followed him out the door. I had no idea what my brother was walking into going over there to tell Janice this news, but I was damned well going with him. Something must have went down between Derrick and Janice sometime after he left my house and us getting over here, I say that because we were met in Janice and Derrick's driveway by her even finer than her sister Terri, who was frantic!

CH. 29

JANICE...

I was thinking that this day couldn't possibly get any worse when my doorbell rang. I expected to see my sister Terri but I could have died when I looked out of my peephole and saw Terri, Marvin and his brother Anthony. I opened the door in total shock. What's going on, I asked nobody in particular? You tell me, Terri answered as sarcastic as ever. Please tell me again why I always call her, when I only regret it almost as soon I do it, I thought to myself? Terri has nothing to do with us being here, Marvin answered. Well what does, I asked him almost frantically? Janice there's something that I must tell you, Marvin replied. Marvin this is not the place or time, I said as Derrick came down the stairs asking who was at the door. I stepped aside and let Terri, Marvin and Anthony all come into view. Derrick had a look on his face as if he had seen a ghost or two, maybe three. Everyone was silent but the air was so thick that you could cut it with a knife. Of course my big mouth sister was the first to break the silence. What the fuck is going on here Janice, she asked. Why were you crying on the phone and why are your eyes all red? Before I could get a word in edgewise she was in Derrick's face, asking what did you do to my sister you faggot? Who in the fuck are you calling a faggot bitch, Derrick shot back? I nearly jump out of my skin as I ran across the room and got in front of Terri. I don't know where I got the nerve but I did. Don't you dare call my sister out of her name in my house, I yelled! Ain't that a bitch, Derrick replied you didn't say a damn thing about her calling me a fucking fag did you? Well if the shoe fits I began to say as Marvin gently pulled Terri and me away from Derrick. Janice calm down baby, he said. Baby, Derrick repeated. It's just a figure of speech, said Marvin; just a figure of speech my ass, Derrick answered. Well now that we're all here said Derrick; maybe Janice would like to tell me how long she's been fucking Marvin. No motherfucker Terri, yelled why don't you tell us just how long your faggot ass been fucking Anthony, that's what we want to know? None of this is your damn business Terri, Anthony yelled in her direction. Anything that has to do with my sister is my business, Terri yelled back at him. Finally Marvin spoke up, will everybody please calm down for a minute, he said. You're right Terri agreed with him after all this can't be good for the baby. I'm sorry Marvin said to her I didn't know that you were pregnant Terri. She's not said Derrick, Janice is. At that moment both Marvin and Anthony turned and looked at each other in shock. Is there something wrong, Terri asked? Oh yes there's something very wrong Derrick spoke up. Yeah I said finally getting around to confronting Anthony, I bet you didn't know that Derrick was expecting a child did you, I asked? Janice there's something that you need to know, Marvin interrupted. Not now Marvin, I answered irritated as hell that he had the nerve to but into my conversation. Yes now, he said sounding just as irritated as I was. He was really getting on my nerves now trying to defend his brother. Can't it wait Marvin, I asked? What's so important that you have to keep interrupting me, I asked? No he answered this can't wait; we have to discuss this right now. Wait a minute, said Anthony. I couldn't believe this, first it was Marvin now it's his brother. Who in the hell do they think that they are to come here uninvited for whatever reason and start dominating the whole conversation? Janice please, said Anthony can I have a second with Derrick in private? Why do you need a second with me Derrick asked with a very concerned look on his face? Because Anthony answered, Marvin knows the truth Derrick, I told him today and I suspect that's what he's about to tell Janice. What truth are you talking about Derrick asked, looking as if he was about to kill Anthony. The truth about you and I Anthony answered I told him everything Derrick. At that moment everything went silent as Derrick walked into the living room, sat down on the sofa and buried his head in his hands. What in the hell is going on here, I asked? If you will let me I will explain, well at least try to explain this to you as best I can, said Marvin. The two of you looked peculiar when Janice's pregnancy was mentioned; Terri said does that have something to do with what you have to talk to her about? Yes, said Marvin as a matter of fact it does, but first I need to talk to Janice alone. There's nothing that you can't say in front of my sister, I said. I don't know about this Janice, he said. This is very personal and could be very embarrassing to you. Is it more embarrassing than your brother pretending to be you and climbing in bed with me, I asked, nothing can be more embarrassing than that and I told her about it so whatever this is about it can't be any worse. I'm afraid that it is he said in a way that made me feel real uncomfortable. Finally I gave in and asked him to step into the kitchen so that we could discuss whatever it was that was making me feel so uneasy.

CH. 30

MARVIN...

I should have known better. How could I have been so stupid, one minute I'm standing there in the kitchen telling Janice that the man she's been sleeping with can't possibly be the father of her child? I thought that she was just looking pale from the initial shock of finding out that Derrick was born a woman. I for a moment totally forgot all about the fact that I had just learned that she was pregnant when all of a sudden she passed out hitting her head on the refrigerator on her way down. I tried to grab her as fast as I could, but I was too late she hit her head as hard as hell on the corner of the fridge, and then she hit the floor. She was bleeding from the side of her head. My God, yelled Terri as she ran in, what happened? Derrick and Anthony came running in behind her wanting to know what happened also. I was too busy calling the paramedics. We were talking; she fainted hitting her head on the fridge I explained to the lady on the phone and everyone in the room all at the same time. Don't move her; I said repeating the instructions that were being given to me on the other end of the phone. The paramedics were there before we could blink, so we all followed them to the hospital. What did you tell her, Terri asked me as we were following the ambulance? That's not important right now Derrick spoke up. I wasn't talking to you, I was talking to Marvin she snapped back at him. Please this is not the time or place for this, said Anthony. You're right I agreed plus it's something that Janice has to tell you herself Terri, I said. I know how close the two of you are but still this is a very sensitive situation. We share everything, she said to me. How sensitive could this be? It's worse than you can ever imagine I told her. I apologize, I said once again but Janice has to discuss this with you herself. I guess she finally understood because she didn't ask me anymore questions. The rest of the way to the hospital was relatively quiet. We were in the waiting room for what seemed like an eternity before the doctor finally came out and told us that Janice would be fine

They said that we would be able to see her very soon. Terri was the first one to go in but it was a matter of minutes before she came back out and motioned for me to come in also. I walked in and saw her lying there with her head all bandaged up and tears instantly came to my eyes. I'm so sorry baby I said, I tried to catch you but I wasn't fast enough. It wasn't your fault she replied; it's just that I started to feel dizzy and then when you were telling me that Derrick was born a woman and all it was overwhelming. What, yelled Terri frantically! Anthony told Marvin that Derrick was born a woman repeated Janice. How in the hell is that possible, Terri asked? I don't have all the answers to that I told Terri, Janice has to talk to Derrick for herself but there's one thing that I do know and that is that the baby you are carrying is mine and not Derrick's. Terri looked as if you could've knocked her over with a feather. I never even asked you how the baby was doing. I apologize. The baby's fine Marvin she said, but I'm not keeping it. The hell you're not, I yelled, there's no way in the hell you're going to kill my baby! Marvin please calm down, said Janice. How am I supposed to calm down when you're talking about killing my baby and for what reason just because it's not Derrick's. That's not the only reason she said, I don't even know you that well Marvin. You knew me well enough to fuck me but you don't know me well enough to have my baby, is that what you're saying to me Janice, I asked? I have to get some air and a drink of water, Terri said excusing herself from the room still looking shocked. Marvin please try to see things from my side; Janice continued. I wasn't trying to hear it though, I didn't give a fuck how all of this was going to play itself out, but I knew one thing and that was this; No one was killing my baby. Janice I interrupted before she could get another word out of her mouth. I think that you need to talk to Derrick before you can even begin to make any decisions ok? I don't want to talk to Derrick ever again in life, she said. Baby you have to, I told her walking over to the bed and leaning down to give her a big hug. Will you be here with me, she asked? If that's what you want, I answered. That's what I want she said, I can't handle this alone Marvin, Terri is all I have and I damn sure don't want my mom or hers knowing anything about this. At that moment the doctor came in followed by Terri; He told us that they were going to keep Janice overnight for observation and to make sure that the baby was ok. Are you the husband, he asked? No I'm not, I answered but I am the father of the child. Would you like to stay the night, he asked because if you do, we can have a sleep cart brought up for you. I would like that very much, I replied. I will let the others know, said Terri reaching over and giving Janice a kiss on the cheek as she walked out of the door.

CH. 31

DERRICK...

Yesterday had to be the worst day of my life. I went to see Anthony and found out that my fiancé Janice had been sleeping with Anthony's twin brother, and because he and his twin had some fucked up unresolved issue from their past, that Anthony had slipped in bed with Janice and tried to fuck her too. I also found out that she has known about Anthony and me for quite some time, and has never said a word to me about it. It's not that I didn't already know that she was fucking someone behind my back; after all she is pregnant isn't she? I know damn well that I didn't get her pregnant, it's biologically impossible. Then Anthony goes and betrays me by telling his brother that I'm not a man after all and to top it all off they all show up on my doorstep, Anthony, Marvin and the bitch Terri. I could have dropped dead right there in the living room, when Anthony pulled me in there and told me that he had told Marvin everything that I had confided in him. As I realized that was what Marvin must have been telling Janice we heard a loud crash come out of the kitchen where they were talking. Anthony and I ran in there to find Marvin and Terri standing over Janice while she lay unconscious bleeding from her head. If something happens to her baby, I will never forgive myself. I know that it isn't mine but she has wanted a child every since I met her. I knew that it was the one thing that I couldn't fake. I could afford the best strap on penis that money can buy. I know it feels just like the real thing because I've had plenty of women before her tell me so. Janice is the only one that has never looked under the covers and saw it yet, I guess that's why I've been with her longer than any other woman. I always pretend to come just as she comes that way we're both wet and she can never tell the difference. If it's one thing we women can do and do well its fake an orgasm. I can fake a penis and a nut but I can't fake a conception, no way, no how. After all the bullshit that I've put her through, she deserves some happiness. My thing is that I came home to tell her myself but instead I got into a long drawn out fight with her about my pride being bruised by the whole baby situation. Poor Janice she had no idea what she was up against. I have been so unfair to her. There's no wonder she found herself in another mans bed. Then again who am I lying to, myself? I was never going to tell Janice that I was a woman. How do you tell that to another woman that you've been sleeping with for almost two years that you know would never willingly sleep with another female? I guess that I pretended to be a man so long that I had forgot that I wasn't. That was until Anthony came along. We were attracted to each other right from the start. The poor thing thought that he was having gay tendencies and I think that I fell in love with him at first sight. I knew that it was foolish of me to come clean with him, while in a man woman relationship. I wasn't even completely honest with him either; I told him that Janice was just a roommate that I would have liked to break the news to before we could completely be together. Damn I didn't think that Janice would cheat on me though but hell why not? I was cheating on her, right? I want to talk to her more than anything but according to her bitch ass sister Terri, Janice never wants to see or speak to me ever again. Oh yes she couldn't wait to come out of the hospital room and give me that tid bit of news. Oh yeah and I could have killed that Marvin motherfucker when he announced to the doctor that he was the baby's father. Ain't that a bitch? If it wasn't for his big mouth ass brother, he couldn't have been so fucking sure. The worst part about all of this, is I'm so confused now I don't know what I want. I love Anthony, but I love Janice also. If only I could talk to her without arguing, I could try and straighten some of this shit out. I mean, I know that she has a million questions after all, who wouldn't? I don't care if she wants to see me or not, I'm going to that hospital and I'm going right damn now.

CH. 32

JANICE...

I was confused when I first woke up this morning. I had no idea where I was, or how I got there. Then just like always reality started seeping through the cracks of my memory. I remembered how Derrick and I were having this big fight and he slammed me on the bed rather hard. I was terrified so I called my sister. I just wanted to get out of there and away from him at first, but I had to let him know that I was aware of what he was doing behind my back with Anthony. Well thank goodness that I never got around to that part because I had no idea what or who Derrick was or is at that point. That saying what a difference a day makes continues to take on a new meaning for me everyday lately. One minute I'm answering the doorbell, positive that it's my sister and the next minute I'm waking up in the hospital. Yes you heard me right, waking up in the hospital with my head all bandaged up, finding out that I've been a lesbian for the past couple of years. Let's not forget the showstopper; I'm pregnant by a man that I hardly even know. I can't blame anyone but myself for the latter one though. After all I am a grown woman. I should have known better than to sleep with Marvin unprotected. That's just it though, I never intended to sleep with Marvin the first time, and the second time I had convinced myself that I was already pregnant by Derrick which I now know is completely impossible. It just happened is not going to cut the mustard for me. It just happened my ass, things just happen once, Marvin and I, we just happened twice. Now he's insisting that I keep the baby, but I'm not sure about that. I'm not sure about anything. How could I have been so stupid? How could I not be able to tell a woman from a man? What is wrong with me? I guess that explains why Derrick never let me perform oral sex on him. He told me that he was shy about his body and I believed him because I was shy about mine. I guess that's why being with Marvin, excited me so much I just loved the way that he would strip naked in front of me and take all of my clothes off. We would rub and touch all over each others body and it made me feel so alive like I hadn't been with a man in years. Truth be told, hell I hadn't. Now that I think back on things what man doesn't want to be orally pleased, especially after he does you so well? I don't ever want to look Derrick in the face again. Actually it will be embarrassing as hell. What right does he have to invade another person's life like this? There should be a law against people doing something like this to anyone. Then again I should have taken some time out to learn a little more about Derrick. I should have known things like where he was from or did he have siblings? I should have known something about his background before I not only jumped in bed with him, but moved him into my home. What was I thinking, shit he could have turned out to be something worse, like a serial killer or a child molester. How in the world can I bring a child in the world that I'm going to be responsible for taking care of and keeping safe, when I can't even look out for myself? If it wasn't for Terri watching out for me all my life, there's no telling where I would be by now. Poor thing she has her own life a husband and a child to worry about. But nevertheless she's always here for me, to hold my hand and help me out of the many messes that I manage to get myself into. I could never thank her enough. It was hard enough when she was just my best friend, but now that she's my sister it's even harder trying not to disappoint her. I know that she must be thinking that out of all the foolishness that I've managed to get myself into, this tops it all for sure. Well, well, well guess what the fucking cat just drug in, here comes this bitch Derrick walking into my hospital room with some damn flowers, the nerve of him. I know damn well that someone must have told him that I never wanted to see or talk to his ass ever again in life.

CH. 33

TERRI...

I've been on the phone all morning lying and making up excuses to my boss, my mom, Janice's mom and my husband. I can't believe what I found out yesterday myself let alone try and explain it to someone else. I always knew that Derrick was a lying cheating dog. I didn't know that he was a lying cheating female dog. And he had the nerve to call me a bitch, ain't that a play on words. I see he has forgotten where in the hell he came from. I have a million questions for Janice's ass. How in the hell do you not know a woman's body from a mans'? Derrick must be one ugly ass bitch because he doesn't look like any helluva good looking man to me. I definitely can't imagine seeing him as a woman. Marvin tried to explain what little he had found out from his brother about the situation to me. I was hearing him but not listening much. It seemed like I just couldn't keep a train of thought for the life of me. I swear that my mind was bouncing all over the place. Once he got me back to Janice's house and to my car, I don't even know how I drove myself home. I barely remember dragging myself into the house. Somehow I found my way to the shower and ended up falling asleep on the sofa. Before falling asleep, I peeked into my bedroom and just like I figured, Todd and Brandon were fast asleep. I didn't want to risk waking Brandon up I had already had the day from hell, I didn't want to follow it up with the night from hell. I woke up the next morning with my head aching, so I go grab an aspirin. I can't even imagine what my sister is going through right now, so I hurry into my bedroom and grab some clothes out of my closet. I wish Todd had let Brandon spend the night at my moms. My mom is on her way to pick Brandon up. I asked her to keep him for the rest of the day. She came right over and picked him up. She could feel that something wasn't right with me; it took everything I had to get her out of here, without her getting a full confession out of me. Marvin called and asked if I had spoken with Janice today? I told him that I hadn't. He said that he had been trying to reach her room all day and all he was getting was a busy signal. I told him that I had no idea why Janice wasn't answering her phone but that I was on my way to the hospital as we speak. He asked me if I wanted to ride over there with him and Anthony. I told him that I would rather drive my own car and why did Anthony want to go to see Janice anyway? I hung up and tried calling Janice's hospital room myself. She answered on the second ring. I asked her if there was anything that I could bring her and she said no. she told me that Derrick had been to see her and that she had ordered him to leave. She said that she had even threatened to have security physically remove him in which case, I wish that they would have. Who in the hell does he think that he is? I told him last night that she didn't want to see his sorry ass anymore. What else does he want from her for Gods sakes? I called the number on the caller I D Marvin had called me from. I told him that Derrick had been to see my sister and could he please ask his brother to tell him to stay away from my sister. Why did he do that, asked Marvin? Are you asking me, I replied how in the hell am I suppose to know, I answered? What's wrong I heard Anthony ask in the background? Marvin told him that Derrick had been to see Janice after I had told him that she didn't want any contact with the queer whatsoever. I didn't hear what Anthony said in return because Marvin got back on the phone with me and informed me that they were pulling into the parking garage. I told him that I was on my way also, as I hung up the phone, grabbed my car keys and ran out the door as fast as my legs could carry me.

CH. 34

MARVIN...

After Terri informed me that Derrick had been to see Janice this morning, it felt as if Anthony's car couldn't park fast enough for me. I will personally kick his or her ass if he upsets her any more than she already is. I swear if anything happens to my baby all hell is going to break loose for real. My brother even agrees with me about that. Anthony tried to calm me down as best he could. She was sitting on the side of her bed eating a bowl of soup, when we finally reached her room. Hello beautiful I said, as I walked through the door. She looked up and continued to eat her soup. How are you feeling today sweetie, I asked? I feel like someone dropped a ton of bricks on my head, she said. I heard that Derrick was here earlier, I said. I noticed that tears had begun to develop in her eyes and roll down her face. Why are you crying, I asked her? I just wish that everyone would go away and leave me alone, she replied. How can we do that, I asked? I don't know just do it she said, as she started to sob out loud. I went over, sat on the bed and put my arms around her. I just sat there and let her get it all out. Anthony stepped out of the room to give us some privacy. I will never leave you alone, I said to her. I feel horrible, she said. You took a nasty fall I said to her; anyone would feel horrible after that. It's not just the fall Marvin, she said. I thought that I was carrying my fiancé's child and it turns out that I'm carrying your child; my fiancé turned out to be a woman, which makes me a lesbian. I stopped her right there; first of all I said you had no idea that Derrick was a woman, so you didn't willingly have sex with a female. What difference does that make; she asked looking into my eyes? It makes all the difference in the world, I said to her. It's not like you did it on your own free will, you were tricked into it and that's not fair to you, but it's not the end of the world and you're definitely not a lesbian. You're just saying that because I'm your friend and you like me right, she asked? The reason I'm saying it is because, I love you and it's the truth, I answered. How can you love me when you haven't even known me that long, she asked? I didn't know that there was a time limit on loving someone, I said but I definitely know how I feel. My whole life has been turned upside down Marvin; she said I don't even know where to begin my life from here. Let's try to begin it together, I said to her. That will happen over my dead body, said Derrick stepping into the room. I stood up and stopped him from coming any closer to Janice. Please leave Derrick this has nothing to do with you, I said to him. I think you've got the situation twisted he said to me, you are the one that doesn't have anything to do with this it's between Janice and me. There's nothing between you and I, Janice yelled at the top of her voice. I guess Anthony must have heard her yelling because he came running in, as soon as he saw Derrick and I standing face to face he stepped in the middle facing Derrick. What are you doing here Derrick, he asked? I came to talk to Janice Derrick said to him. She doesn't want to talk to you, Anthony replied. Why don't we leave and give them some time to themselves. I'm not giving your brother anymore time with my woman, Derrick stated. I'm not your woman you sick, twisted, freak, Janice yelled in Derrick's direction. I went over and put my arms around her to comfort her and to quiet her down before the staff came in and threw us all the hell out. What in the world is going on in here, Terri said finally arriving. I could hear my sister screaming clear down at the other end of the hall, she stated. She wants Derrick to leave and he's refusing, I answered her. I'm going to get security or I'm kicking this he she's ass out of here myself she said, which one is it going to be? Terri wait, Janice yelled! What am I waiting for, Terri asked her? Let's handle this without calling in any outsiders and without any ass kicking please, I'm embarrassed enough by this situation as it is, she added. You have nothing to be embarrassed about honey, Terri said to her. If anyone should be embarrassed, it's Derrick. I love her Derrick said looking at Terri as if he could kill her right now with his bare hands. What do you mean you love her, asked

Anthony am I invisible here? I don't love you, Janice said to him because I'm not a lesbian and I wish you would not only leave here but stop by on your way and get your shit out of my house. Where am I supposed to go Janice, Derrick asked? You can go live with Anthony, back where you came from when I met you or just plain go to hell for all I care Derrick, she replied. I'm not leaving you, Derrick said to her. What do you mean you're not leaving her Derrick, Anthony cut into the conversation once again, have you forgotten about us, he asked? No I haven't forgotten, said Derrick starting to cry. His voice started to sound strange and scary; it was flip flopping from a high pitch to a low tone, as if there were two voices coming from one body both male and female. It's just that I've fucked up her life and I don't know how to fix it he continued in that same mixture of tones. You can start by leaving now and letting her get some rest, said Terri calming down. The nurse came in at that very moment and asked everyone to leave so that Janice could calm down. Anthony asked Terri if she could give me a ride home and she said yes. Terri and I waited to hear from the nurse. Finally she came out and told us that Janice had been given a mild sedative and that it was best for her and the baby to rest now. We left immediately afterwards. Terri drove me home and I asked her in to have a drink with me to discuss the situation at hand.

CH. 35

ANTHONY…

I was worried that Derrick was on his way to having another nervous breakdown. I took Marvin to the hospital hoping to run into Derrick there because I had been trying to reach him all night long to no avail. I was standing out in the hallway, when I heard Janice yelling at the top of her lungs. I hurried in to see what all the chaos was about and there was Derrick. He was going on and on about how much he loved Janice and how sorry that he was about ruining her life. If I hadn't gotten in that room when I did, he and Marvin would've probably torn each other apart. I managed to somehow get in between them and calm the both of them down. The baby that Janice is having is Marvin's and I'm about to become an uncle. I'm ecstatic about that but as I was saying Derrick kept going on and on not making any sense at all. He had told me in the past that he once suffered a nervous breakdown to the point that it landed him in a mental institution. That's why I convinced him to come home with me. I convinced him to come out of drag for once and for all. It was high time that Derrick died and Carmen came back to live in the real world again. She agreed and took all of that crap off. She took down the braids that hung almost to the middle of her back. She took off the men clothes and sneakers, and I took them out to the dumpster. She was standing in the bathroom mirror brushing her beautiful wavy hair into a ponytail, when I returned, walked up behind her and kissed her on the cheek. She smiled and turned to face me with the prettiest hazel eyes that I have ever seen in my life. Are you ok, I asked? I'm not sure, she answered. I really fucked up Janice's life, she replied. I know that you care about Janice honey I replied but she is Marvin's responsibility now, and if you would just leave them alone they will find a way to work it out, I added. I don't want anyone else screwing her over like I did, said Carmen. Marvin loves her, I said and he loves that child she's carrying, believe me he's not going to let anyone harm her; you don't have to worry about that. Carmen took a long hot shower. I gave her two over the counter sleeping pills and put her to bed for a nap. I came out of the room, closing the door behind me. I went over to the table picked up the phone and called Marvin to check on Janice's condition. Much to my surprise Marvin and Terri was across the street, at Marvin's place. He told me that Janice was so upset by Derrick's presence that she had to be sedated. I asked him was that safe for the baby and he told me that the nurse assured him that both mom and child would be just fine? I told him to open the door because I was on my way over. He said ok and hung up the phone. I looked in on Carmen, she was sleeping quite peaceful, so I grabbed my keys and headed across the street. Marvin made me a double cognac and I sat down on the sofa next to him. I never thought that I would give a damn said Terri breaking the silence but is Derrick ok? Her name is Carmen, I said to her and yes she's fine. She's had a nervous breakdown in her past and I was afraid that she was having a relapse, I said to her. Excuse me but I have a hard time imagining Derrick as a woman, said Terri. I understand I said to her, but you will never see Derrick, as you know him again. I thought that you said that he was asleep over at your place, Terri asked? Carmen is asleep over at my place, I answered Carmen and I both agreed that today is when Derrick will die forever and Carmen will be reborn to face reality. What is she going to do about work, asked Marvin aren't they use to a dude occupying that desk? How is some chick going to show up for work Monday morning without some questions being asked? Are the two of you ready for that, Marvin asked? Personally I want Carmen to go back to school and pursue a career in teaching because that's what she really has a passion for but it doesn't really matter to me. I'm prepared to have her back no matter what she decides to do, I said to him. Did the two of you stop by Janice's place and collect his things, Terri asked? No Terri, I answered her as a matter of fact; I was going to ask if you would do me a favor and get rid of all that stuff for me. I wouldn't know what to get rid of, Terri replied. That's easy said Marvin; just throw away everything that belongs to a man. I'll drink to that, said Terri looking as though she had already had one drink too many.

CH. 36

JANICE...

Despite all of me and Terri's efforts to keep them from finding out my mom and Mrs. Faniece still found out that I was in the hospital. They both showed up first thing this morning demanding to know what was going on. I had no choice but to tell the truth, at least as much of the truth as I could. But I started from the beginning telling her all about the night that I met Marvin and saw Derrick kissing Marvin's brother, all the way to me finding out that Derrick was really a woman. My mom nearly fainted but I warned her against it. I told her that it's the way I got my self in here in the first place. As we were talking Marvin and Terri walked in. Terri introduced him to everyone of course his good looks and great manners spoke for themselves. My mom wanted to know how the baby was doing and I told her that so far everything was fine. She got around to whispering in my ear, that Marvin was the finest man that she'd ever saw. Can you believe that there are two of them, I whispered back. It's not polite to whisper, said Terri jokingly. Finally after reassuring themselves that everything was fine they left. How did they find out that you were here, Terri asked? Probably my job, I replied. I'm glad that you told them everything because I wouldn't have known where to begin, said Terri. I know that you're the glue that holds this family together, I said, but it's time for me to stand up on my own two feet. So now you're going to take my second job, Terri joked? No I'm not taking it I replied, well maybe partime, I joked. I get to go home tomorrow, I said. I'm happy to hear that, said Marvin. Oh there's something that I have to tell you about Derrick, said Terri. Drop it on me, I said. I didn't think that she could tell me anything worse than I knew already. She told me that Anthony and Derrick had decided to cut the Derrick disguise out completely and introduce the world to Carmen, as if it were just that simple. Here's a man that I've loved and lived with for almost two years and they're just going to wipe him off the face of the earth just by throwing away some clothes and some sexual devices? The more I thought about it the more ridiculous the whole situation seemed, it was as if I had been having a sick nightmare for a very long time and was slowly coming out of it. What does Carmen look like I asked? I would say that I haven't seen her but on the contrary we both have, she said. I asked her what was she talking about and she said; do you remember that day when we went over to Anthony's to try and get some answers about him and Derrick? Yes I answered, what about it? Do you remember that attractive young lady that we saw Anthony leaving his condo with, asked Terri? Please don't tell me that the woman we saw was Derrick, I said in total shock. Yep you guessed it, said Terri. Oh my God she's beautiful, I said. She didn't even look remotely like Derrick I said. Well that was her, Terri said and to my understanding you'd better get used to seeing her around because she and Anthony is scheduled to get married next month. I'm not ready to see something like that, I said. I figured as much, said Marvin. That's why when Terri and I went over to your place to get rid of all Derrick's things, I brought over some of mine, he said. Why on earth did you do that, I asked? Because I'm not letting you or my child out of my sight, said Marvin and I knew that you staying over at my place was a bit much right now? This is happening a bit too fast for me, I said. There's isn't anything too fast about it, said Marvin you are not ready to be by yourself right now. As a matter of fact between my baby and me you may never get another day alone again. I smiled rather weekly, feeling very tired and sleepy. It must have shown because Marvin started adjusting my pillows for me to lie down. He gave me a kiss on the cheek and pulled the covers over me as I drifted off to sleep. I'll be here to pick you up and take you home tomorrow, he said. Goodnight sweetie, I heard Terri say. Goodnight Terri, I was asleep before she could close the door.

CH. 37

CARMEN...

Anthony thought that I was asleep, but I wasn't. I heard him on the phone talking to his brother. I'm guessing by the way that he grabbed his keys and ran out the door that he was in a hurry to tell Marvin about my transition from Derrick back to Carmen. I'm glad that he got me out of that hospital room though; believe it or not I was on my way to another nervous breakdown. I remember regaining those old feelings from back when my ex-husband cheated on me with that bitch. I remember my heart beating so fast, and not being able to breath, the next thing that I know I was locked away in a mental institution, being fed pills breakfast, lunch and dinner. That's when I vowed that no one would ever hurt me like that again. That was my vow to myself and I plan on sticking to it until the day I die. I'm sorry that Anthony has to be caught in the middle of all this but he will only have his brother to thank for his broken heart. I can't believe that he feels as if it's justifiable for his bitch ass brother to fuck my woman and get her pregnant. I know that I was dishonest with her, but that was my situation to clear up. I just wish that Janice would have come to me with what she saw that night. I don't know how in the hell I was going to explain to her why I was kissing a man in the mouth, but hell I would have tried. I'm not surprised though that instead of her coming to me, she gets with the bitch Terri who hates my guts and goes spying. That's how she ended up meeting that bastard Marvin for the second time, and now not only has he taken my woman but as if that isn't enough she's having his child. Anthony expect us to just clean this entire situation up by me getting rid of Derrick and being Carmen after all of these years. I suppose that next he will propose that we all become one big happy family. Yeah right that shit will happen over my dead body just as I said before. Anthony I can live with, after all he's a sweetheart that's why he so easily forgave his brother for sleeping with his fiancé all those years ago. What kind of brother would do something like that to another? I will get his ass though; he can do what he wants to Anthony but not to me. I will hurt his ass in the worse way, a way that will make him wish that he were never born, and while I'm at it, I will pay back Janice and Terri too. I will get everyone of them back if it's the last thing that I do. I wrote Anthony a note telling him how sorry I am and that I must leave before I cause any more trouble. I told him that I love him from the bottom of my heart and that I always will. As sad as it sounds, the truth is I do love Anthony just not as much as I love Janice. I don't even believe it myself, but when I was standing here listening to Marvin talking about how he was sleeping with her and that Anthony slipped in bed with her, I could have killed them both with my bare hands. All I keep thinking about in my head is the way she humiliated me at the hospital. She was acting like she hated my guts. I could imagine that it's hard for her, finding out that she's been sleeping with a woman all this time, but what about what they did? I know that she must have been terrified finding out that the man that had slipped in bed beside her wasn't Marvin, but Anthony. I really can't say how Janice feels about anything anymore, after all I didn't think that she would sleep with another man behind my back but she fooled me didn't she? I'm not at all surprised that she didn't even have enough sense to protect herself, but she had enough sense to lie to me about it though didn't she? She stood right there and looked me dead in my eyes and swore that she hadn't been sleeping with anyone else. I had even begun to entertain the thought of her being raped or something. I swear if she would have told me that, I would have believed her and all the time she was over there rolling in the hay with Marvin. I'm so glad that everyone's underestimating me the way that they are. They all think that we're about to be one big happy family and that's the end. I'm so sorry to disappoint everyone but the party is just beginning.

CH. 38

TERRI...

I picked up Brandon and headed home to wait on Todd. I felt guilty that I had not been much of a wife or mother these days. Todd's the best husband in the world though; he's very understanding about the way that I am, when it comes to Janice. I suppose that his background plays a significant part in the way that he feels about our relationship (Janice's and mine) that is. An elderly couple adopted Todd at birth. They never hid it from him though; as soon as he was old enough to understand they told him the truth. They also kept all the information that they had gotten from the agency about Todd's biological parents for him. Therefore he didn't have to do a lot of senseless searching for them. Unfortunately for him by the time he was interested in locating them, they were both deceased. It wasn't long after his adoptive father died of a massive heart attack that a couple of months following his mom passed away also. That's why he's so committed to Brandon and I. We are basically all that he has in the world. I love the fact that he truly understands why I'm so overprotective of Janice, because we're all that we have. We have our mothers and our stepfathers but we are much closer to each other. Curtis our good for nothing biological father could care less, if we were dead or alive. My poor son Brandon has either been with a sitter or my mom for the past couple of months. I wouldn't be surprised if he no longer recognized me at all. Damn that Derrick/Carmen person. This shit is so confusing to me. How in the hell are we suppose to accept Derrick as some woman named Carmen? I suppose that Anthony feels that just because it's so easy for him to forgive and forget, it's suppose to be that easy for us all. I mean why wouldn't it be easy for him after all he knew the truth all along we were the ones in the blind right? Poor Janice, she's finally gotten away from that asshole and here he comes right back into her new life, it's just not fair. I look at the clock and realize that now I've been waiting for Todd a little over two hours, this is not like Todd at all. I picked up the phone and dialed Todd's cell phone number; surprisingly it went straight to voicemail. That's really odd; Todd will answer his cell phone no matter what. I sometimes joke with him about even answering it from the grave. I don't bother leaving a message instead I hang up and call the office. I was shocked when his receptionist picked up being that it was way after office hours. I guess she was working overtime or something. I didn't even bother to ask once she told me that Todd had left work, headed for home hours ago. Call me crazy but at that very moment I got this feeling in the pit of my stomach as if something had gone terribly wrong. I passed it off as nerves and lack of sleep and tried and tried to get it out of my mind. My mind went back to the hospital as I wondered if Marvin had picked Janice up yet. He and I had gone over to her apartment and removed anything that looked as if they belonged to a man. They (Marvin and Janice) had decided to move into her place and sell Marvin's place. Even though she would have to get used to Derrick still being around as Carmen, nobody wanted to have to see his ass every time they walked out of their front door. Marvin loves that child that Janice is carrying with all his heart; despite all that's going on right now, Janice and that unborn child is all that he talks about. Anthony on the other hand is more concerned with Derrick or Carmen or whatever it is calling itself these days; well anyway he's more concerned with that person's state of mind. I have to admit that it crossed my mind a time or two also, but with my sister and her unborn being at stake here, my main concern is the same as Marvin's and that's my sister's and her unborn child's. Again my mind went back to my husband and how late he was. I can't wait to tell him about all this drama that's been going on. I'm really anxious to tell him about Derrick really being a woman. I know that he's going to think that I've lost my mind or that my imagination is in overdrive or something. I smile as I imagine in my mind how his face is going to look when I hit him with this. Something like this could only happen to my gullible ass sister. I remember seeing a talk show about women being in relationships with guys and not knowing that the guys that they were seeing were born women and vice versa. I was sitting there yelling at the TV. How could you not know dummy! It's true what they say about things looking much clearer when you're on the outside looking in, if this would have happened to anyone else, a friend, a co-worker or someone like that, I would not have believed them. I would have sworn to God that they had to know the truth all the time. Isn't it funny that some things just don't seem real to you until they hit home? I admit that I thought of Derrick as a lot of things, but a woman was just not one of those things. I thought of him as whorish and maybe even a bit feminine at times. I could've easily believed that he was one of those down low brothers, but a woman, never. I mean after all he did stress over those long thick braids, faithfully having them done every two weeks and all just like a female. Even with that I never saw the full fledged woman thing coming, no way, no how. Janice was so convinced that she thought her unborn child was his; he had her just that fooled. I still wonder how he pulled that one off. She admitted that she never physically saw his penis; he told her some crap about him being shy. I still don't see how he pulled it off that would have been a red flag for me. What idiot has sex with a man and doesn't look at the dick before the man puts it in? I remember her a while back asking me what I thought of oral sex, and of course me thinking of Derrick as the ultimate man whore telling her that she better not be thinking about putting her mouth on him. Janice just laughed and said that Derrick wouldn't let her so much as touch his penis, let alone suck it. Damn, there was another red flag that I overlooked. I should have known then that there was something unnatural about that bastard. What grown man doesn't want head, but hell what grown woman still says penis? Then a scarier thought came to my mind and that is; what do we really know about Derrick, even now? We know that he's really a she right? Dammit even right now at this moment I can't even stop calling the bitch Derrick. How do we even know that Carmen is even her real name, shit to be honest, we don't. In all actuality we don't know anything about this woman or what she is capable of. She's lived in my sister's house as a man when she's really a woman; we know that much. She's carried on a relationship outside of Janice's house as a woman with Anthony. I wonder if he's ever done a background check on the broad, to see if she's telling the truth about anything. I doubt very seriously if he's given it a thought. Anthony's so in love with that broad, she can tell him anything and he will believe it. I don't think that Janice has even so much as met his parents. As a matter of fact I know that she hasn't, because she would have told me if she had. I thought back to when all of this began, I do remember her saying that she was going to drop all of his belongings off at his parent's house, so maybe she has met them and just haven't gotten around to telling me. I'm going to make that background check top priority first thing in the morning. Todd where are you, I say thinking out loud as I dial his cell number for the hundredth time. Once again it goes straight to voicemail, and once again that ache in the pit of my stomach returns. I hang up the phone and head for the kitchen to put on a pot of coffee. I knew that it was going to keep me up, but I don't plan on getting any rest tonight anyway. I'm definitely not going to bed until my husband walks through that door. There's so much that I have to tell him, and so much to sort out. I'm certain that we will be up till wee hours of the morning. I pour my second cup of coffee and carry it into the living room, where I curl up in Todd's favorite chair facing the window. I continue to stare out desperately looking for some sign of Todd's car crawling into the driveway. Todd never came though and sometime after the third cup of coffee, I must have drifted off to sleep from sheer exhaustion.

CH. 39

MARVIN...

I arrived at the hospital around noon to pick Janice up and take her home. She wasn't in her room so I sat down on the chair in the corner to wait. Finally she appeared, being pushed in a wheelchair by a nurse. Is there something wrong, I asked nervously? Everything's fine, the nurse answered; we had to have some routine tests done before discharging our patient, that's all. How about the baby, I asked, is the baby ok? Yes, answered Janice the baby's fine. Why is it that I have the strangest feeling that once this baby gets here I will definitely be put on the back burner? I promise you that will not happen, I said to her while crossing my fingers behind my back. Well that is unless we have a daughter, I added. What does that mean, unless we have a daughter, she asked? Well I said you know that Anthony and I don't have any siblings, just each other. Our parents always wanted a girl, but unfortunately, our mom had so many complications birthing us that she had to have a complete hysterectomy shortly there after. So their dream of having a little girl went up in smoke. Neither Anthony nor I have ever been married, so there hasn't been a daughter in law yet. What do you mean yet, I asked? I know for sure that remark doesn't need an explanation, he said, a granddaughter would make them lose all of their natural minds. I don't think that you, Anthony or I would mean squat to them if they get one, I said. Don't get me wrong they will love a grandson just as well but I think that we both know the effect that a little girl is going to have on this entire family. Well with our family, said Janice it was just the opposite. All they had was two girls, Terri and I so when Todd came along and then Brandon, that kind of evened things out a little. I wouldn't know the effect anything is going to have on your parents, she added because I haven't had the pleasure of meeting them yet. I can take a hint, but I told her not to worry her pretty little head off because as soon as the doctor gives the ok; we you, me and our unborn will head straight for my parents place.

CH. 40

ANTHONY...

I arrived home expecting Carmen to be sleeping peacefully; instead I found that she had left. At first I thought that she may have been in the bathroom or something, but after checking the garage I found that her car was gone also. My first thought was maybe she had gone back over to the hospital to try and talk to Janice again, which I hoped that she hadn't. I was thinking that I have to stop her from going there and ruining Marvin and Janice's new beginning. The last thing they need right now is for her to show up with her drama. I love Carmen dearly, I swear that I do but what she did to Janice was down right wrong. What I did to Janice wasn't right either, and I must apologize sincerely from the bottom of my heart for that. Janice is such a sweetie; I swear I couldn't have asked for a better sister in law. Well she's not my sister in law yet, but I'm sure that Marvin will take care of that little technicality real soon. I called the hospital to see if Carmen had gone there. A nurse answered the phone and said that Janice had been discharged around noon and had left with Marvin. I was taking off my jacket and trying to clear my head when a piece of paper lying on the dining room table caught my eye. I picked it up and tears began to flow from my eyes as I read Carmen's apology/good-bye letter. The letter went on to say how sorry she was for messing up so many lives with her deceptive behavior. I cried harder when I read the part about her never coming back. I can't believe that she could just leave me like this. I love her with everything that's inside of me, doesn't she know that? Why would she leave at a time like this, when we've finally gotten everything out in the open? There are no more secrets, no more sneaking around and most of all no more lies. I made myself a drink, sat on the sofa and cried harder. I thought back to the time when I first met Carmen and all the great times we had together. I thought about how much fun it used to be sneaking around together, until Marvin saw us together that day when she was in disguise and came to the conclusion that I was gay. That thought kind of brought a smile to my face, me gay, how absurd is that? I should have known that Carmen was lying about the lady that she was living with just being a roommate though. Nobody cares that much about what a roommate thinks enough to postpone their lives right? Still I never would have guessed in a million years that she was fucking the lady though, or even sleeping in the same bed with her, for that matter. I honestly think that in her state of mind, she thought that she was in love with both of us. The way that she acted in the hospital was so irrational, voices changing inside of her back and forth from a man to a woman's that shit really threw me for a loop. I suddenly began to worry about Carmen's state of mind. I don't even know if she was completely cured from her nervous breakdown. Shit, now that I think about it, I really don't know anything about this woman except what she's told me. I don't even know where to begin looking for her, but there's one thing that I do know without a doubt, and that is; I refuse to interrupt Marvin and Janice tonight.

SIX

MONTHS LATER...

JANICE...

Today is the happiest day of me life, my husband and I are on our way to the hospital. Yes, you heard right Marvin and I were married about four months ago. I guess after all that drama I went through finding out that my live in lover was really a woman that was engaged to my husband's twin brother Anthony. I even thought that I was pregnant by her; I never in a million years would have believed that the child I'm carrying wasn't Derrick's until I found out that it was biologically impossible. Well anyway after the smoke cleared Marvin had insisted that we get married. I would have resisted a little while longer, so that we could get to know each other even better, after all I've been through, but then my sister's husband Todd went missing one day never to be seen or heard from again. I realized how short life with someone you love can really be. It's like magic when someone truly loves you in spite of all your faults, that's something worth holding on to. We didn't have a wedding Marvin and I. Actually we just went down to Vegas tied the knot, and came back home. Once the baby's born we will throw a big reception with all the bells and whistles to satisfy everyone else, because the two of us couldn't be happier than we are right now at this very moment. I never saw two people that were more in love than Terri and Todd, that's why Terri will never believe that he just up and left. I felt guilty that she spent the last months that she had with her husband, mixed up in the mess I had made of my life. Sometimes I even feel guilty being so happy, while she's so miserable. She tries so very hard to put this front up as if she's ok, but I know her all to well and I know that she's dying inside for closure if nothing else. I wish to God that I could give it to her. She doesn't know it but Marvin and I even hired a private investigator to aid in the search for Todd. Unfortunately he couldn't pick up a trail on him. Todd hasn't used any credit cards, opened or closed any accounts or anything, it's almost as if he just walked out of his office one day and literally dropped off the face of the earth. One good thing came out of it though, that Derrick/Carmen or whatever that freak of nature is calling itself these days, left Anthony the same day. I could care less about finding him though; Anthony tried and I'm glad that he couldn't, after all he deserves better than her deceptive ass anyway. I felt genuinely sorry for Anthony at first, after that he she left him, so I drove over to the address that he had given me some time ago when we first started dating. It was supposed to be his parents' home with whom he was supposed to be living with at the time. I wasn't even surprised to find out that it was a fake. The house was one of those boarding homes, which rent out rooms to people in need of a place to stay, and fortunately enough for them they hadn't heard from him since my stupid ass took him in. I catch Marvin staring at me from the corner of my eye. What are you looking at, I ask blushingly? I'm looking at the most beautiful woman in the world; he answered the same as he always does whenever I ask him that question. Marvin reaches over to give me a kiss as I pull up to the red light and stop, when all of a sudden the car to left of us comes straight at us at top speed. The last thing I hear is Marvin yell Janice! I recognize the driver as Derrick in a split second, as I realize that there is only one thing that I can do, to make things right...

EPILOGUE...

MARVIN...

ONE YEAR LATER...

It's been a year now since I buried my wife and daughter. Funny I never believed in true love, let alone love at first sight until the night I met Janice, even though at the time I was just out to score as usual. I didn't score that night though, but I guess in the grand scheme of things I really did. I got to spend time even though it was short; with a wonderful woman that I truly loved and that truly loved me back. I still smile sometimes when I think about how fast she ducked down when she saw Derrick's car pull up that night. I thought for sure that she was just making up an excuse not to go out to breakfast with me when she told me that his punk ass was her man. I have wished a million times in the past year that was really the case. Why couldn't we have already pulled off, before that son of a bitch pulled up? Why is it that just when you feel things can't get any worse for you, they somehow get ten times worse? I was so devastated at the thought of my brother being gay. How I wish to God that was all I had to worry about right now. I swear that even telling my parents would be a piece of cake. It's just not fair that everything in my world had to be turned upside down? Why did our lives have to be altered like this just because one asshole couldn't deal with reality? I wonder when Carmen decided to kill us. I also wondered if she planned on killing herself, or was it fate when she rammed into Janice's car, that day. One moment we were driving down the street as excited as we could be about seeing an ultrasound picture and finding out the gender of our child, and in the blink of an eye my wife and child are dead. Derrick and I say Derrick because I guess that's who he was that night. I mean after all he did have on his Derrick disguise. Janice was pronounced dead on arrival. Believe it or not, I only had minor injuries. My wife in the last minutes of her life threw her body over mine. I wish to God that I had been the one driving that day, and could have thrown myself over her and my daughter. I would have gladly given my life for theirs. Once again tears began to uncontrollably fall from my eyes as they do so often this last past year. Janice said that she wanted to help her sister Terri find closure for the loss of her husband Todd. Ironically as it may sound she did, because his body was found in the trunk of Derrick's car. I thought that Terri was going to have a heart attack and die, when she saw what was left of her husband, in the trunk of that car. I wonder where in the hell was he keeping that car with a dead body in the trunk. The smell was unbearable. If there truly is a silver lining around every cloud as they say, I guess it would be that Terri and Anthony ended up being a couple. They moved into Anthony's place a couple of months back. My parents are so in love with Brandon that they don't know what to do. It goes without saying how torn up they were over the loss of their daughter in law and unborn granddaughter. My daughter was buried in the casket with her mother; she was the most beautiful thing that I had ever seen in my life. Terri's husband Todd was buried right next to them; we had the funerals together. I don't even know where to start picking up the pieces of what used to be my life, not even now. I pour myself a drink just like I've done everyday for the past year, and sit and stare out of the window.

COMING SPRING 2010…

KNOW HIS VOICE
BY
AUNTIE ROBYNAN

DIALOGUE;

I can't believe this is happening to me, sitting here having to even be in the same room with this low-class basement stripping broad. If stupidity was a crime I'd probably spend my life in jail, if not for beating the hell out of this scary ass trick, then definitely for being bothered with that trifling, stinky breath, nasty feet, only wash his ass when he wants to fuck but ugly nigga Titus. I don't even like ugly guys and this one is tore up from the floor up and nasty as hell on top of that. But you know how the game goes when a nigga is flashing cash in your face all the time. What else is there? There's a saying that goes; hoes will do something strange for a piece of change, and the sad part about that is, they will. They will lay up under the nastiest, stinkiest, most trifling, disrespectful or just plain no good for nothing misfit. They will moan, groan and even tell them that they love them, all the while lying through their teeth, and the worse ones are the ones that don't even need the money, like my dumb ass. I knew that I had no need for this low life, back in the days want to be. He knew that he was just a sucker and I was literally sucking him dry, or so I thought. Anyway back to this broad in here trying her best to player hate after all I've been through. Her name is Tara and she was one of Titus's little stand by's that I ended up getting into a fight with. She had the nerve to show up on my doorstep like she was bout it, so you know what I did, I handled my business. I beat her ass to a pulp. I just don't get this broad; I got in this shit for the money. I did get me a new Lexus and a two-hundred thousand dollar home built from the ground. My infant son and I wear the best of everything. This broad lives in the heart of the ghetto, on a block that has maybe three or four raggedy houses still standing, she drives an old beat up Toyota and dresses cheap as hell. Therefore for the life of me I can't imagine why she would want to confront me about this loser that I only use for cash. Come on ladies you know what I mean. I'm sure all of you ladies out there that are truly on top of your game know exactly how to get in these want to be balers pockets. Of course when he can't afford the best, go ahead and mingle with the rest, cause you gone pay over here baller. Can you feel me ladies? At the end of the day though who's the real winners and who's the real losers? Why don't you come on this journey with me, and let's find out together...

CH. 1

Hi my name is Deanna and in this book I will be the so called balleret, (terribly mislead materialistic female) just like a lot of my mislead sister out here in the world. Anyway I was just minding my own business one hot summer day, mad as hell because I'm pregnant, miserable and I have a heartache. My baby's daddy thinks that I'm two kinds of stupid or something because lately I never have any idea where in the world this nigga is. I've called his mama's house a million times and she keeps answering talking about she doesn't know where he is. That's some bullshit if I ever heard any, and I had no problem telling her so. The bitch had the nerve to tell me that even if she did what would it have to do with me. Usually I'm good at playing these childish games with her and can come right back at her, but right now I'm too hurt because I really love this man that suddenly wants to be a boy now that I'm carrying his child, and I thought that he loved me to. But I don't know, maybe I've dogged Elroy, that's my baby's daddy to the point of no return. Speaking of Elroy he is one fine diamond in the rough, he has this pecan colored skin that just melts my heart, and please don't mention those light gray eyes of his, and he has a body to die for. I could go on for days talking about how fine Elroy is, but there's a down side to every story and his flip side is, he doesn't have anything. He has a little piece of a job, but what's that? After paying the bills and buying household necessities we barely can afford a night at the movies. Although we're always at every opening night showing of whatever strikes our interest. I mean he doesn't have any major duckies, and I'm about to have my first child. Nope that job just isn't going to do the trick, I need more. I'm twenty five with my associates in nursing and Elroy works at different factories doing general labor. I used to think that was good enough, after all we were getting by. I'm not even sure that I want to be tied down except for the fact that I'm stuck with Elroy's baby. I got a lot of nigga's on me like crazy but they don't got nothing either. I mean they not dead broke, just broke according to my standards. My girl Sonia now that's a real ballerete, that nigga she got Hakim got money up his you know what, and he really loves that girl. They have a house out in the suburbs with an in ground pool and everything. They got a new baby; she has more clothes and jewelry than any one person can ever wear in a lifetime, now that's what I call real love. That's the kind of love I want. Hakim is one of the biggest drug dealers in our city; he's ugly as sin though. Sonia on the other hand is as pretty as she can be. I'm not funny or nothing like that but she can have just about any man that she wants. She's short, almost as thick as I am, that means in all the right places, she has the prettiest light brown eyes and shiny long black hair that hangs down her back. But that Hakim is really hard on the eyes if you know what I mean. I swear if you look at that man too long you might break out in tears. He's about three hundred and fifty pounds on a five foot five frame, black as night, cockeyed and got the nerve to wear an afro. He has the nerve to hit on all of her friends behind her back. Believe it or not, my girl doesn't even sweat it though; she says that every time she catches him it costs him plenty. That's what I'm saying girl, that's how real playerettes play the game. So why do I have all of these lames, I ask myself? I had this one nigga named Simon, he owns his own plumbing business, that's ok I guess. But really though how far does he think that's going to get him; playing in other people's do-do, ain't no real money there. I asked him to buy me a pair of three hundred dollar shoes from Gucci one day, and he responded like I had called his mama a bad name or something. Then there's Roger, he has a great job, but he's like thirty going to college with teenagers, who got time for that? Somebody should have told him that he was supposed to go to school when he was a kid, plus he was cheap as hell also. Then there was this other guy, what's his name? All he ever wanted to talk about was church and God, if you want to believe in all that stuff go right ahead. But please don't smother me with it because I don't have time for it. Anyway as I was saying, I'm hot, miserable and I need something cold to drink. The phone starts to ring and I go to answer it. Guess who, my number one lame Elroy. What are you doing pretty lady, he asks? What am I doing, nigga are you serious, I answer back. For one I'm carrying you're child, while you are probably out all night with some trick, I say to him in a sarcastic tone. I can't believe that after all I've done for you; now that I'm pregnant all you seem to do is come home just long enough to wash your behind and change clothes, I add. He told me that he didn't feel like hearing this right now and I told him to bad because he was going to hear it anyway. He replied that he wasn't and hung the phone up in my ear. I couldn't believe that he hung up on me so I checked to see what number he had called from, his mama's of course, I should have guessed that much, the nerve of this loser. I called back, but didn't get an answer. What do I do now? I don't really associate with my other male friends anymore. I almost forgot about this one guy George that I was really into last summer. He was the perfect boyfriend, minus two major flaws; one he had a girlfriend, a live in at that. They've been together for about twelve years, got a couple of kids too. Seems to be the perfect family, but don't they all? The majority of these so called relationships seem so great when you are on the outside looking in. But if you take a closer look into these circuses they call marriages and relationships these days, it's enough to scare you into finding JESUS. No disrespect to the man upstairs because to him goes all the glory. Second flaw real quick one and don't laugh; little bitty weenie man. Now that is nothing but frustration, but hey if the price is right we will deal with that to. Ladies why do we do things like this to ourselves? We will even marry someone we're not satisfied with, and we wonder why so many marriages end in divorce. Maybe because there wasn't any love there to begin with. Never ever marry for anything less than love. Please if you don't hear anything else in this book at least hear that. Let's not go to hell for something so silly. I know personally because like a fool I tried to tolerate it, and ended up cheating with Elroy. George claimed that really hurt his feelings. But in all fairness, I gave George a year to leave that broad, since he claimed that she made him so miserable. But he had every excuse in the world why it just wasn't the right time. I mean this man had more excuses than a nigga going to jail. He claimed that she didn't have any family here. Then it was that she didn't have sufficient employment like I did, and he just couldn't throw her out on the streets with his children in tow. But as soon as he saw that I was getting serious about Elroy, everything changed. All of a sudden he was willing to ship her to Alaska if that's what it took. But all that showed me is that he could have gotten rid of her all the time if that's what he wanted to do. He just kept running game on me as long as I tolerated it; every man that cheats runs that same game. Always remember that whatever you are willing to tolerate, you will never change. Therefore please stop settling for second best or anything less. Anyway I wasn't about to leave Elroy alone, so we broke up, George and I. I sent that lame on back to Suzy homemaker. The real truth is; he had never left her anyway. Back to me being as hungry as a hostage, I called Simon's cheap behind. He may not buy me three hundred dollar shoes but at least he can feed me, this is why I can't see myself ever being with someone like him. He's really a nice looking guy, with a great home on the other side of town. He's a real down low creep move, if I must say so myself. The phone starts ringing again. I answer and it's Elroy again asking me have I eaten anything today as if he cares. I told him that I was going to walk around the corner to the store and grab a soda and a bag of chips, so call me back later and make it a lot later. This time I hung up on him. The nerve of him acting all concerned about me eating when he doesn't even come home at night, and when he does it's four or five o clock in the morning, screw him right now I have other plans. I call Simon and ask him to come and take me to that new corned beef joint that everybody's been talking about. He said that he would be right over and that he was anxious to ride me in his new Cadillac truck. I couldn't help thinking what was this cheapskate doing with a Cadillac truck and he couldn't even buy me a pair of Gucci loafers. I know he don't got no major money like that, he must got good credit or something. I told him that I would see him when he got here. I'm going to try and talk that lame into letting me grip that so that I can drive down Elroy's mama's street. Once he spots me driving a Caddy truck maybe he will come to his senses and forget that stupid job and start hustling like a real man. I'm sitting over here pregnant, jobless and my transmission is gone in my car thanks to Elroy driving it way out to that stupid job. Now he's treating me like a dog, not even coming home at night. But you know what; pregnancy ain't nothing but a temporary position. As soon as I have this baby I'm gone dog the hell out of him right back. Speaking of pregnancy, I better hide this stomach. I'm twenty two weeks, but you can't tell. I throw on my cute white shorts, and after a little effort they actually zip half way up. My top is oversized, so you can't see that I even have a stomach. I have my hair cut low because it's hot as ever out here, and I definitely have the best hair stylist in the city. I put on my sandals, grab my matching handbag and I'm out of here. I wait on the porch because this central air is killing me.

www.ingramcontent.com/pod-product-compliance
Lightning Source LLC
LaVergne TN
LVHW091557060526
838200LV00036B/883